JOINT CUSTODY

JOINT CUSTODY

An Alternative for
Divorcing Families

MEL MORGENBESSER
AND
NADINE NEHLS

ILLUSTRATIONS BY PAT ROSEN

Nelson-Hall nh Chicago

To our parents

LIBRARY OF CONGRESS CATALOGING IN PUBLICATION DATA

Morgenbesser, Mel, 1946-
  Joint custody.

  Bibliography: p.
  Includes index.
  1. Children of divorced parents—United States.
2. Custody of children—United States. 3. Parenting—
United States. 4. Divorce—United States. I. Nehls,
Nadine, 1952- joint author. II. Title.
HQ777.5.M67   306.8′9   80-22182
ISBN 0-88229-620-5

Manufactured in the United States of America

10 9 8 7 6 5 4 3 2 1

Contents

Acknowledgments

We appreciate the interest and assistance of those who helped us complete this book. We are especially indebted to Dennis Trudell for his careful and creative editing of this manuscript. We are also grateful to the following people: Connie Ahrons, Kristine Auler, and Carolyn Dawson of the University of Wisconsin, Madison, and Kathy Jeffords and Ann Milne from the Dane County Family Court Counseling Service. Their valuable suggestions helped us to more clearly and completely present our ideas. Thanks also go to Gloria Barsness who quickly and pleasantly typed and retyped all of our drafts.

In addition, we are indebted to the many people who were willing to talk with us about the subject. We especially wish to thank the parents and children who shared their personal experiences with joint custody; without them we and others could not have learned as much.

And finally we will always be grateful to our friends and family members who continually asked, "How's the book going?" To these special people—many, many thanks.

1

Why This Book

Custody—few words arouse more emotion to hundreds of thousands of divorcing parents each year. Divorce in itself is a difficult and stressful experience. Recently dozens of books have been written which attempt to help people recover, adjust, and even emotionally profit from the experience of divorce. The popularity of such books attests both to the increased number of people divorcing and to the numerous problems associated with it. When children are involved, the divorce process becomes even more difficult, confusing, and painful. While there are many reasons for this, there is little doubt that one major dilemma in any divorce involving children is the need to answer the difficult question of who shall have custody. There is no other issue in the divorce process which has the potential to create more problems.

When one looks superficially at how couples handle the custody question, it may appear that either the decision is made easily, or a long, potentially destructive custody fight ensues. However, upon closer examination, we often find that even for those couples who initially handle the custody issue with apparent ease, the resulting decision can be a source of problems for years to come. For those couples who become involved in custody fights during their divorce, the process becomes infinitely more difficult and emotionally draining. It is no accident that custody disagreements are called fights and battles. The participants are parents and children, and it is a war in which everyone loses.

While we believe that most people reading this book would agree that no one wins in a custody fight, few might realize initially that no one really wins in any custody decision. Superficially, custody appears to be a win-or-lose proposition, where one parent's gain is the other parent's loss. After all, the parent who is awarded custody has the total legal right and power to decide how the child will be raised. While the noncustodial parent may have visitation rights, the dominant control clearly lies with the parent who has legal custody. In fact, the noncustodial parent, stripped of his or her right to actively participate in the child's development, often begins to look more like a visitor or playmate than a parent. If one goes to any shopping mall, park, or zoo on a Sunday afternoon, one is likely to see numerous noncustodial parents trying desperately to parent their children, but often only succeeding in entertaining them. How, then, can we maintain that custody is not a win-or-lose proposition? Hasn't the noncustodial parent lost, having been deprived of the legal right to actively participate in his or her child's up-bringing? Hasn't the custodial parent won, who retains such rights? Although this certainly appears to be the case on the surface, a closer look reveals that the parent with custody has also suffered losses. For example, this parent often finds that he or she faces increased financial, physical, and emotional responsibilities. In most cases, parents who have custody soon realize that they now have one less person with whom to share the responsibilities of childrearing. Custodial parents are forced to make important decisions about the children alone. They may have no other available resources should an unexpected problem or crisis occur. Furthermore, parents who have custody of their children must often make detailed arrangements in order to secure any private time for themselves. Perhaps an even greater difficulty is that following the divorce, custodial parents usually find their child having increased emotional needs and demands, to which they alone must respond. Essentially, the parent who has custody has lost a partner with whom to share the responsibility for childrearing.

The child involved in the divorce process has also, of course, suffered significant losses. Although we will discuss this phenomenon in more detail later in the book, a brief comment is necessary at this point. No matter to what extent divorcing parents try to prevent it, questions arise. "What is going to happen to me now?" "Did I cause my parents to break up?" "Do I have to take sides with one parent against the other?" "Will I be abandoned?" These questions are often asked by children of divorced parents. In many divorce situations, children feel they have lost a parent. These common questions and doubts indicate a child's confusion and concern during and following a divorce, and to a certain extent they are natural and healthy. Yet an unhappy custody arrangement can intensify them into more serious concerns.

Because traditional custody decisions often result in significant problems for all involved, it is crucial that we examine creative ways of handling the issue of custody. What we will introduce and discuss in this book is a new alternative to traditional sole custody. This option is joint custody, a nontraditional form of custody which may be desirable and appropriate for some divorcing families. Joint custody insures both parents the legal right and responsibility for raising their child or children following their divorce. This custody arrangement may be a means of minimizing some of the losses suffered by parents and children involved in divorce. We will explain what joint custody is and how to decide if it is an appropriate alternative for you and your children, and we will discuss the benefits and problems in-

volved in such a decision. Information about how to imple-
ment this custody decision in your own divorce is included,
as well as interviews with men and women who presently have
joint custody.

Perhaps as important as *why* we are writing this book is
how we hope to write it. Many books aimed at the public
try to promote a central idea or theme. Many of the recent
"how to" books are good examples of this tendency. We do
not pretend to believe that joint custody is an appropriate
solution for all divorcing parents. Similarly, we do not claim
that joint custody is a panacea for all of the problems associated with divorce. We do believe that it is a custody option
deserving serious consideration and that it may well be a
preferable alternative to sole custody for many divorcing
families.

In order to help the reader decide if joint custody is an
idea worth pursuing, we will attempt to provide the most
accurate and complete information available. Since joint
custody is a recent phenomenon, there is little research from
which specific facts can be cited. Consequently, we will include related studies and theory as well as anecdotal material in helping you make your own informed decision.
Discussion about the relative merits and problems of joint
custody will continue for many years, but we attempt here to
provide the reader with current information concerning this
innovative and controversial custody option. We expect that
three groups will find this information especially valuable:
divorcing families interested in learning about options to sole
custody; divorced families who have informal, nonlegalized
custody arrangements similar to joint custody; and professionals, particularly in the legal and mental health areas, who
work with divorcing families.

2

Custody Decision Making — Past to Present

When one looks at the overall divorce picture in the United States today, the significance of custody decision making becomes obvious. In 1976 there were over a million divorces in the United States—a *million divorces* in one year (United States Vital Statistics Report, 1977).

The divorce rate has doubled during the past fifteen years. Today one out of every three marriages will end in divorce. Even more significant to our discussion is the growing number of children affected by this; the one million divorces in 1976 directly involved over one million children (United States Vital Statistics Report, 1977). There appears to be no reason to believe that either the number of divorces or the number of children involved in them will decrease in the near future. Divorce has certainly become one of this country's most significant social realities, and we must find ways to deal creatively with the circumstances that it presents.

One of the major dilemmas of divorce is the issue of child custody. Most people reading this book probably have little knowledge of how custody decisions have been made in the past. Consequently, they may assume that the question of custody has always been decided as it is now. More likely, many may feel that a historical overview of custody decision making is of little importance—that what is significant is what is happening today. However, far from being a mere tour of the past, even a brief history of custody decision making will provide us with a better understanding of how we came to where we are, as well as some ideas about the direction we are headed.

According to ancient Roman law, a father had the right of control over his children (Myricks, 1977). This control included the right to sole custody in the event that a marriage was terminated. The basic philosophy of paternal control, or *patria potestas,* was continued under English common law until the fourteenth century (Alexander, 1977). This rule "was followed by *parens patriae,* which meant the King would protect all who had no protector" (Alexander, 1977:377). During this time the father still retained control over child custody. The basic assumption was that the father was entitled to the services and earning of his children as compensation for his liability for their support and maintenance (Foster and Freed, 1978). Children were viewed as property, and until the early nineteenth century males had supremacy in the ownership of property.

In 1839 the United States abandoned the notion of what could be called "father's dictatorial control" (Alexander, 1977). The passage of married women's property acts in the nineteenth century brought a willingness to grant equal power over the children to both parents (Bondehagen, 1977). According to American Law Reports, when both parents wanted custody the courts often awarded divided custody. Because children were still considered chattel, divided custody generally meant alternate placement of children, not equal parental rights and responsibilities.

It wasn't long until the courts changed their position on divided custody. People involved with custody decision making began to look at it with disfavor, arguing that custody was best vested in one parent. Thus by the mid-nineteenth century, custody was usually awarded to the mother.

> As our culture became both urban and industrialized, the father worked away from the house and left the raising of children, for all practical purposes, in the hands of the mother. (Roman and Haddad, 1978:37)

The mother gradually came to be seen as the preferred parent. As previously mentioned, today custody is still awarded to the mother in the majority of all divorces (Sheresky and Mannes, 1972).

You may have noticed that although the law changed in 1839, the basic issue still centered on parental rights, not those of the child. Children were in many ways viewed as property; thus to a large extent custody decision making revolved around the question of ownership. When there were disagreements about custody, the rights of the parents were the central concern. It was not until 1889—in what remains the most far-reaching, significant change in custody decision making—that the rights of children were considered as paramount. Chief Justice Brewer of the Kansas Supreme Court declared in a landmark decision that "the paramount question in any custody case was what would best promote the welfare and interest of the child" (Foster and Freed, 1978: 331). This concept was reaffirmed by Justice Cardozo in New York in 1925. These and subsequent legal decisions shifted the emphasis in custody cases from parental rights to those of the child. The crucial issue in custody decision making today remains what decision will be "in the best interests of the child." The importance of this "best interests" concept cannot be overstated. It is the principal guideline from which custody decisions are currently made.

Virtually every parent involved in divorce, and certainly every parent involved in a custody disagreement, has had to deal with the very difficult question of what is in the

best interests of the child. The issue is not only problematic
for parents; it also perplexes lawyers, judges, and experts in
child development trying to develop criteria to help answer
this question. When guidelines have been developed, they
have tended to be broad and thus difficult to apply in specific cases. Although each state has its own definition of "in
the best interests of the child," there are many similarities
between them. For example, consider the Wisconsin Statutes
(1977), Section 37.247.24 (lm) which reads as follows:

> In making a custody determination, the court shall con-
> sider all facts in the best interest of the child and shall
> not prefer one potential custodian over the other on the
> basis of the sex of the custodian. The court shall consider
> reports of appropriate professionals where admitted into
> evidence when custody is contested. The court may con-
> sider the wishes of the child as to his or her custodian. The
> court shall consider the following factors in making its
> determination.
>
> (a) The wishes of the child's parent or parents as to
> custody;
>
> (b) The interaction and interrelationship of the child
> with his or her parent or parents, siblings, and any other
> person who may significantly affect the child's best interest;
>
> (c) The child's adjustment to the home, school, re-
> ligion and community;
>
> (d) The mental and physical health of the parties, the
> minor children and other persons living in a proposed cus-
> todian household;
>
> (e) The availability of public or private child care ser-
> vices; and
>
> (f) Such other factors as the court may in each indi-
> vidual case determine to be relevant.

Now consider the pertinent section of the Colorado State
Statute:

> Section 14-10-124. Best interests of child
>
> (1) The court shall determine custody in accordance
> with the best interests of the child. In determining the best
> interests of the child, the court shall consider all relevant
> factors including:

(a) The wishes of the child's parent or parents as to his custody;

(b) The wishes of the child as to his custodian;

(c) The interaction and interrelationship of the child with his parent or parents, his siblings, and any other person who may significantly affect the child's best interests;

(d) The child's adjustment to his home, school, and community; and

(e) The mental and physical health of all individuals involved.

(2) The court shall not consider conduct of a proposed custodian that does not affect his relationship to the child.

You will notice that the two statutes are very similar and that in both states the court attempts to consider all relevant factors.

One concept often utilized to help the court decide the child's best interest is the idea of parental "fitness." The court will only award custody to a parent whom it deems "fit." In regard to custody, this term means essentially that the parent is capable of providing a physical and emotional environment which will contribute to the child's growth and development. While certainly useful as a guideline, the concept of fitness lacks practical utility. It is general and vague, and it is difficult to apply in specific cases. In fact, within the fitness criteria we encounter one of the many dilemmas of custody decision making—What does one do when both parents are deemed fit? We believe that this is often the case. In many divorces both parents meet the fitness criteria, and both could in fact provide an appropriate emotional and physical environment for their children. Of course, there are a small percentage of cases where one or both parents are not able to provide such an environment for their children. In such cases, the court intervenes and attempts to insure that a custody arrangement is in the child's best interests. However, in the vast majority of cases both parents meet the fitness criteria. The recognition of this fact has led many individuals to challenge the routine practice of awarding custody to the mother. The decisions of judges in custody cases have been challenged by organizations such as Fathers United for Equal Rights and Fathers for Equal Justice. These organizations argue that the process and effects of traditional custody decision making reflect a sex bias.

The increase in frustration over custody decision making and the demand for alternatives to sole custody are rather recent occurrences. When one looks for causes or contributory factors to them, many possibilities exist. We believe there have been at least three societal changes which have resulted in the demand for innovative custody arrangements such as joint custody. These are the women's and men's liberation movements, the growing number of states granting no-fault divorces, and the increased willingness of the public to demand that the legal system be sensitive to their particular needs. For some couples these changes will result in custody fights; for an increasing number of others, joint custody may well provide the desired alternative.

Women's and Men's Liberation

An extensive analysis of the changing roles of men and women in the United States is beyond the scope of this book. However, both the women's and men's liberation movements have contributed significantly to the development and demand for joint custody options. Though there is a great deal of debate as to the overall effect of the liberation movements, there can be little doubt that both have had a rather profound effect on childrearing in general and custody in particular.

"As the 1970s began," Barbara Deckard writes, "the myth of the American woman as the 'happy housewife heroine' conflicted increasingly with reality" (Deckard, 1975:322). She also notes that more and more women began to work at paid jobs, and statistics bear her out.

> Between 1950 and 1974 the number of women workers
> nearly doubled while the number of men in the labor force

increased by only one fourth. (United States Department of Commerce, 1976:26)

Between 1960 and 1974 the number of women working continued to increase significantly.

Table 2-1
Percentage of Women in Labor Force

Age	1960	1974
20–24	46	63
25–34	36	52
35–44	44	55
45–54	50	55

Source: *A Statistical Portrait of Women in The United States.* U.S. Department of Commerce, Bureau of The Census (April 1976: p. 30).

While single women (never married) have historically had higher percentages of employment than other women, this group as well as the "other ever married" group (which includes the divorced) did not drastically increase their percent in the labor force from 1960 to 1974. Rather, the most significant increase in the percent of women employed occurred in the "married women, spouse present" group. The chart below illustrates this phenomenon.

Table 2-2
Marital Status of Women in Labor Force
(Numbers in Thousands)

Marital Status	1960	1975
Single	5,401	8,465
Married, spouse present	12,253	21,111
Other ever married*	4,861	6,932
Total	22,515	36,508

*Includes widowed, divorced and married, spouse absent. Source: *A Statistical Portrait of Women in The United States.* U.S. Department of Commerce, Bureau of The Census (April 1976: p. 30).

There are several possible explanations for the significant increases in the percentage of employed married women. First, it may be an economic necessity for most families with children to have two incomes; more than one working adult is perhaps becoming the norm for the typical, childrearing American family. Second, couples with two incomes may be more able to afford child care, whether it be a baby-sitter, day care, or nursery school; this in turn allows both adults to pursue outside employment and its associated benefits. It is also possible that married women with children feel more motivated to seek employment because of the potential to share childrearing and basic household responsibilities with their husbands. However, while this potential exists, surveys show that where both the husband and wife work, the woman retains most of the childrearing and domestic responsibilities she had prior to outside employment.

The fact that fewer divorced than married women have entered the labor force also deserves attention. Like her married counterpart it is often economically essential that a divorced woman with children have outside employment. However, the lack of a second income or sufficient child support may not make it worthwhile for a divorced mother to work outside the home. Many such women may be forced to accept welfare type payments, since that may be more profitable than working and paying for child care. Certainly a divorced woman with custody of one or more children will find it difficult to work outside the home and care for the children. These factors may contribute to the less significant increase in the percentage of divorced women entering the labor force.

It is difficult and also beyond the purposes of this book to offer a further, in-depth explanation for why more married than divorced women have entered the job market. What we do hope to make clear is the obvious fact that women, whether divorced, married, or single, have expanded their roles. It used to be said that the availability of child care services would draw women away from the family. It is now obvious, however, that regardless of the degree of governmental support for child care, women are going to work (*Business Week,* 5 February 1979:16). Women are demanding activities and job opportunities in addition to or in place of childrearing and domestic tasks. This assertive push has also resulted in the demand for sharing of responsibility between living partners. Raising children, traditionally an exclusively female responsibility, is being viewed by more and more individuals as a joint responsibility. Although in many families where both spouses work, the female retains most of the childrearing and household tasks, there is still a growing trend for men and women to share these responsibilities. This trend has undoubtedly contributed to the demand for and feasibility of joint custody.

As women have begun to assume expanded roles, a parallel movement now called "men's liberation" has also emerged. Partially in response to the women's movement and partially out of their own needs, some men have begun to question their roles in relation to certain stereotypes. One assumption being increasingly questioned is that men cannot or do not want to be significantly involved in childrearing.

A child custody case with which the reader may be familiar is *Salk* v. *Salk.* Dr. Lee Salk, a prominent psychologist, fought for and received custody of his two children. In this landmark case, the traditional assumption that a mother should have custody of her children unless she is "unfit" was rejected by the court. The decision in the Salk case

> was based on a sprinkling of precedents in other states where courts have recently given custody to the father although the mothers were not found unfit (Dullea, 1976:24)

This case and others like it reflect not only the current questioning of maternal preference regarding child custody, but also the courts' recognition of societal changes and new ideas about parenthood. It is clear that more men are playing a more active role in raising their children. This is evident both in marriages and, increasingly, when couples divorce. Like women, men are redefining and expanding their roles. Many are questioning their assumed role as breadwinners and are instead looking at new and varied lifestyles which do not focus solely on a commitment to a career.

Androgyny is a concept which reflects these changes. This term is receiving increased attention today, in part because of the women's and men's liberation movements. The word androgyny means both male and female. Sex role stereotypes reinforce traditional perceptions of male or female attributes and behaviors.

> In contrast, psychological androgyny (Andros, male and Gyne, female) allows men and women to be "both" independent and tender, "both" assertive and yielding, "both" masculine and feminine. In other words, psychological androgyny expands the range of behaviors available to everyone. (Bem, 1977:318)

There is a growing realization that childrearing is not necessarily inherently more satisfying to women than to men.

> As women have begun to speak out about their lack of total fulfillment in caring for the family—saying that meeting the needs of children and a husband does not necessarily lead to complete self-fulfillment—there has been a growing recognition that some women want to be deeply involved in mothering and others do not. And some fathers might be more involved in fathering if given the chance. (Sargent, 1977:11)

The concept of androgyny recogizes that both females and males can nurture their children, may wish to do so, and should be permitted to have that opportunity. This notion is certainly harmonious with custody arrangements permitting both parents to remain active participants in their children's lives. Joint custody is one such custody arrangement which obviously does not embrace rigid, outmoded sex role stereotypes.

The men's and women's liberation movements, as well as the attention given to concepts such as androgyny, have undoubtedly had an affect on parenting. Likewise, these trends have also influenced and will continue to influence custody decision making.

No-Fault Divorce

Until 1970, in every state in this country the only way a divorce could be obtained was for one spouse to show that the other was at fault for the breakdown of the marriage. "Fault" generally included either adultery, cruelty, desertion, or drunkenness (Wheeler, 1974).

It was not enough that one or even both spouses had decided they no longer wanted to be married—state law mandated that they needed an "acceptable" reason to obtain a divorce. Although laws differed from state to state, the usual procedure involved one spouse accusing the other of something—often under the general label of "cruelty." Then the other spouse, if he or she also wanted the divorce, did not contest the charge, and the divorce was granted. A distinguishing feature of this type of divorce philosophy, writes Michael Wheeler, is that "to obtain a divorce it is not enough to show that your marriage is dead . . . you must establish that your spouse was at fault for its death and you were free from blame" (Wheeler, 1974:2).

Although state laws differ regarding divorce and custody decisions, there are areas where they overlap. For example, there is always the possibility that in a fault divorce, the grounds for it may be used as a reason for not awarding custody. "If a man is divorcing his wife because she committed adultery, he may claim custody on the basis that her behavior makes her an unfit mother" (Wheeler, 1974:77). A judge confronted with arguments, charges, and countercharges in a contested divorce may be strongly influenced by the divorce proceedings when deciding upon custody. Another potential problem area in fault divorces arises when

one partner wants a divorce and the other does not. The custody of the children in this instance may become a major
bargaining issue. "A husband or wife who wants a divorce
may be forced to relinquish all claims to custody of the
children in order to get his or her spouse not to contest it"
(Wheeler, 1974:79). Because of these problematic areas, we
believe it is clear that the concept of demanding fault as a
prerequisite for divorce can and often does affect custody
decision making.

However, in 1970, a significant change took place in the
area of divorce law. The California Family Law Act of that
year was the first state law in the country to remove fault as
the basis of divorce. Marriages in California can now be terminated if the court finds that "irreconcilable differences"
have resulted in a marriage's "irremediable breakdown."
The concept of ending marriages upon demand, inherent in
no-fault divorce, obviously appeals to much of the public
and is supported by many lawmakers. Eisler notes that "in
less than four years, one out of every three American states
had adopted some form of no-fault divorce, and all over the
country legislatures are considering ways to incorporate this
new approach into their laws" (Eisler, 1977:11).

Although the adoption of no-fault divorce laws does not
necessarily change the way custody decisions are made, it
clearly affects the entire custody issue. First, it removes some
of the problems described above when fault divorce and
custody issues overlap. Second, and perhaps more important,
it recognizes that people have a right to decide for themselves whether or not they wish to be married. No-fault divorce removes the necessity of one spouse being labeled as
at fault for the marital breakdown. A spouse need no longer
be judged cruel, adulterous, or drunk in order for a divorce
to be granted. Inherent in no-fault divorce is the important
idea that two people can end their marriage and still be seen
as moral, responsible human beings. If this is true, as it surely
is in many situations, then it is not difficult to understand

that in such marriages both spouses are likely to be fit as individuals to provide a reasonable environment in which to raise children. Thus we believe that joint custody is in some ways a natural outgrowth of no-fault divorce. As no-fault divorce recognizes and removes stereotypes inherent in fault divorce, so also joint custody helps the recognition and removal of stereotypes inherent in the routine granting of sole custody.

ASSERTIVE DEMANDS ON THE LEGAL SYSTEM

An interesting change which seems to be taking place during the past decade is an increased public expectation and demand that the legal system be more responsive to particular needs. The legal system in the United States has lost some of its aura and mystique. Perhaps it is the general push towards consumerism—a movement which has touched everything from private industry to government—which has encouraged people to demand more responsiveness from their legal institutions. Another cause may be the rash of Watergate-type incidents, which has made people realize that government makes mistakes and is not beyond reproach. Probably it is a combination of these and other factors which has encouraged people to insist that the legal system see them as individuals and their needs as vital. Clearly the impetus for joint custody has come from the public, not from professional organizations, legislatures, or the courts. As the public continues to expect the legal system to be sensitive to individual custody needs, we are likely to see an increase in creative custody decisions.

As we have discussed, society is undergoing monumental changes in areas closely related to custody decision making. The women's and men's liberation movement, no-fault divorce, and the assertive demands on the legal system are causing reverberations to be felt in the entire custody arena. Several examples will help illustrate the effects which these social changes have had on issues related to parenting.

One is the issue of child support. Only a few years ago it was virtually unheard of for a woman to be required to pay support, even when the father had custody of the child or children. Today, "the majority of state laws have made child support the obligation of both parents, rather than as formerly, the primary responsibility of the father" (Freed and Foster, 1977:311). Shared child support is becoming more prevalent as the number of families increases in which both parents work. In the *Chicago Tribune,* Philip Solomon, past president of the Matrimonial Lawyers Association, put it simply in saying, "it is no longer a matter of sex, it is a matter of dollars" (Gunn, 1978:15). The trend toward shared responsibility for child support based on both parents' incomes is in part an outgrowth of the equal rights movement. It recognizes the changing rights and responsibilities of parents in today's society. Suzzane DuVal, of the Department of Health, Education and Welfare's Child Support Enforcement section, believes it logical that as judges are increasingly awarding custody to men, women should help support the children. She adds that "my own view as a feminist is that this is good" (Gunn, 1978:15).

An even more controversial phenomenon illustrating the increased willingness and pressure for men to share in childrearing is the advent of paternal child leave. Many employers, both public and private, have for some time had a policy regarding maternity leave. Often a specified period of time is guaranteed women following birth in order that they can stay at home with newborn children. Recently some men have demanded and received time off following the birth of their child so that they might share in this postnatal experience. Couples have sometimes decided that the father will take a leave of absence from employment rather than the mother. Other couples have requested to each work on a half-time basis, thus freeing one parent to care for the child. Though still far from being the status quo, the concept of paternal leave is but another indication of the trend toward shared childrearing.

Sweden is a step ahead of the United States in regard to paternal leave. The Swedish government has a flexible program which allows men to receive approximately 95 percent of their salary for a maximum of seven months following the birth of their child. More and more men are using this program each year (Shepard and Goldman, 1979).

The awarding of custody has evolved from predominately male dominance to predominately female dominance and now finally to the more recent belief that in many instances either or both parents can appropriately care for their children following a divorce. A thorough understanding of custody today requires that we look closely at contested and noncontested custody cases. A careful examination reveals a great deal about the relation between societal pressures and human behavior. After such an examination, we will better understand not only what happens in custody cases, but why it happens.

Custody Decision Making—Noncontested Cases

In many divorces the decision as to who will have custody of the children is not debated. The custody decision is made by the divorcing parents outside of court, transmitted through their attorneys, and granted by the courts. The fact that the parents arrive at a custody decision between themselves usually makes the best interest of the child issue a moot point. Unfortunately, what often becomes the central issue is which parent is most insistent on wanting custody of the child. Preliminary discussions frequently focus on who wants most to raise the child, not on who could best do so. Superficially it may appear that this is a reasonable way in which to decide most custody cases. After all, it would seem unwise to award custody of a child to a parent who does not want it. This argument appears logical and even self-evident; it is however, far too simplistic. Men and women have been socialized to believe that the mother is the preferred parent. Consequently, the mother is expected to want and demand custody of the child. The mother who decides otherwise is stigmatized by a society believing that a mother's place is with her children. If she feels otherwise, people may ask, "What's wrong with her?" A mother who does not want custody of her children is generally viewed as deviant. As with other deviant behaviors, society tends to stigmatize a person who exhibits it.

A father who wants custody may also face criticism or at least skepticism. Fathers in general are seen as not really being able to provide a proper environment for children. They are frequently viewed as not having the skills necessary to demonstrate tenderness and caring. Fathers themselves may often feel inadequate in this role, and this perceived inadequacy stems in part from the lack of preparation and expectation for performance in childreading. Even if it is acknowledged that a father can provide a reasonable emotional environment, it is presumed that he could not handle the day-to-day childrearing responsibilities such as cooking, changing diapers, packing lunches, etc. Sadly, even if it is agreed that a man has the necessary skills for single parenting, his desire for it may be suspect—he may be viewed as unmanly. Intellectually, we may recognize that these assumptions are stereotypes of men and women in general and mothers and fathers in particular. However, they are powerful myths which have resulted in decreasing the choices a divorcing parent may feel she or he has in the custody decision area. Social norms and mores, not legal and psychological criteria, have dictated the way most custody decisions have been made. There has often been little freedom of choice, weighing of alternatives, or significant options for divorcing parents. As long as there is a pervasive belief that children should most often reside with their mother, custody decision making will in most cases remain relatively routine. Couples will agree outside of court that the mother should have custody of the children; the custody proceedings will be noncontested; and, as is the case today in over 90 percent of all divorces, custody will be awarded to the mother. Although this scenario is still frequently followed, it is by no means the only appropriate option open to divorcing families.

Today there are an increased number of cases in which both parents want custody and have not reconciled this conflict outside of court. There are numerous reasons for this, some of which have been alluded to previously in this book. One obvious reason for the increasing number of custody disputes is the increasing number of men seeking custody of their children. In such instances, the traditional awarding of custody to the mother is often contested.

One drastic and destructive outgrowth of custody disputes is the growing number of kidnappings related to or following custody decisions. In a 1978 article in the *Chicago Tribune,* James Yuenger reports:

> It's estimated that 25,000 to 100,000 child snatchings occur every year, and the number is growing with the soaring American divorce rate. . . . Children's Rights, Inc., a Washington-based lobbying group, estimates that two-thirds of all snatchings are carried out before custody hearings begin, by parents who fear the court will grant custody to the other. (Yuenger, 1978:22)

Anne Demeter (1978) has written one of the few books about this phenomenon. In it she presents a personal account of her children being kidnapped by their father. Ms. Demeter believes:

> Because the kidnapping of a child is a way of "taking" the custody of that child (acting outside of the law), it is important to view parental kidnapping in the perspective of the current legal conventions regarding disputed child custody. (Demeter, 1977:126)

When a custody disagreement or fight occurs, the judge is the person who makes the decision regarding custody. Many judges believe that custody cases are among the most difficult ones they hear. Vague criteria and general lack of information concerning the effects of various custody options, coupled with the importance and longevity of the decision, contribute to the difficulty of adjudicating contested custody cases.

Historically when there have been custody disputes, certain presumptions have been followed. For instance, when both parents were deemed fit and wanted custody, courts adhered to the "tender years" concept. This concept refers to the commonly held belief that a child of a young age should be with his or her mother. Although the tender years were not strictly specified, they usually included the years from birth to school age, and they often extended beyond the early school years. The maternal preference inherent in this concept was supported by early theory and research in child growth and development. This research is being challenged by recent investigations which have examined the influence of fathers on children (Hamilton, 1977) and the experiences of single fathers (Heatherington, Cox, and Cox, 1976; Mendes, 1976; Orthner, Brown, and Ferguson, 1976; Keshet and Rosenthal, 1978). This means that the tender years concept is also being questioned. In fact, according to Foster and Freed (1978), "A recent check of the American jurisdictions indicates that the tender years doctrine has lost ground so that in 1978 it is either rejected or relegated to the role of 'tie breaker' in most cases" (Foster and Freed, 1978: 332).

If the tender years doctrine is indeed relegated only to situations which require a tie breaker, then what criteria is being used to decide the remainder of child custody decisions? The answer is that the first and foremost criteria used in custody disputes remains the "best interest of the child" concept. However, as we have mentioned previously, specifying and evaluating the exact components of this concept is extremely difficult. It is especially complex in cases where both parents are deemed fit. To some extent there is a vacuum in the body of basic theory pertaining to child custody decisions. While the tender years doctrine coupled with maternal preference is being widely challenged, there is little to take its place. Therefore, there are relatively few detailed guidelines upon which courts can base their judgments. The concept of the psychological parent, that is, the parent with whom the child has developed the strongest and most affectionate ties, is receiving increased attention. Yet it is obviously very difficult in many cases to decide to whom a child is most psychologically attached.

The problems involved in deciding custody cases have resulted in a trend in many states to appoint a *guardian ad litem* for the child. A *guardian ad litem* is a person, often an attorney, who represents the best interests of the child. Unlike the parents' attorney (s) , this person does not work for either of the divorcing parents; rather the *guardian ad litem* is appointed by the court and represents the child in the custody proceedings. Behind this is the assumption, supported by many authorities, that neither the judge nor the parents' attorneys can adequately represent the interests of the child in a contested custody case.

It is evident that there are no clear-cut standards in custody decision making. However, Henry F. Foster, professor emeritus of law at New York University, and Doris Jonas Freed contend that in most new statutes the following are often articulated as important considerations when deciding upon child custody:

1. Age and sex of child
2. Wishes of child and parents
3. Interaction and interrelationship of child with parents and siblings
4. Child's adjustment to home, school and community
5. Mental and physical health of all parties (Freed and Foster, 1977:312)

The lack of clear-cut guidelines regarding child custody decisions is an indication of the scope and depth of knowl-

edge about custody in general. At one time in the United
States, custody was granted almost exclusively to the father.
This was a reflection of the social mores and economic norms
of the times. Later the mother was seen as the preferred
parent; this also was influenced by social norms, economic
realities, and later by research in child growth and development. Today the norms are changing, and research is beginning to confirm the contributions and competencies of
both parents in regard to raising children. In part, clear and

well-documented guidelines do not exist because we do not
yet definitely know what types of custody arrangements are

truly in the best interests of the child. Since both parents are often requesting custody today, there may be more contested child custody cases. Perhaps in the near future researchers will provide us with data that will allow us to better understand which types of custody arrangements are best for what ages and types of children. Until then we must be willing to make use of the best information available, coupled with common sense, in the hopes that the best possible decisions are made.

3

What Is
Joint Custody?

Joint custody, as discussed in this book, means that both divorced parents share the rights and responsibilities for raising their child or children following their divorce. As a legal concept, joint custody attempts to guarantee divorced parents an equal say in decision making and in overall child rearing. In such custody arrangements, the crucial issue is that both divorced parents have a right and responsibility for making decisions which affect the child. In many cases, the joint custody agreement stipulates that the child will alternatively live with each parent.

There has been a considerable amount of confusion about joint custody. Perhaps the most frequent assumption is that it always means sharing the child's physical presence equally. Recent newspaper and magazine articles have contributed to this confusion by suggesting that joint custody is an arrangement in which children spend equal amounts of time with each parent. For instance, an article in *Newsweek* magazine begins:

> Every Wednesday morning, the Miyoshi children...
> eat breakfast with their father in his house, then go over
> to their mother's pink house a quarter of a mile away.

1

3

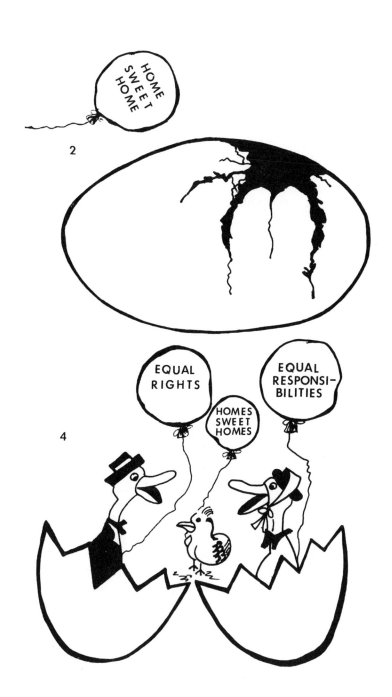

There they stay until Sunday morning when they make the
trip back to their father's again. (Kellogg, 1977:56)

A *New York Times Magazine* article states,

> Six-year-old Tommy Mastin, the central figure in a con-
> troversial childrearing arrangement known as joint cus-
> tody, leads something of a double life in Gainesville,
> Florida. On Monday, Wednesday and Sunday Tommy lives
> with his father at Oak Forrest, a luxury apartment com-
> plex on the city's south side.... On Tuesday, Thursday,
> and Saturday, the boy lives with his mother in the older
> north side neighborhood of 26th Street.... Fridays vary,
> depending on his plans and those of his divorced parents.
> (Dullea, 1976:24)

Charlotte Baum writes in a *New York Times Magazine* article, "Over the past five years, my three children have been
living in two different households. One of them is mine and
the other is my former husband's" (Baum, 1976:44). Although these articles do mention that a central idea of joint
custody is joint decision making and responsibility, they
tend to focus on specific living arrangements. This type of
publicity reflects a tendency to associate joint custody only
with arrangements where the child spends approximately
half of his or her time with one parent and half with the
other. While this is certainly a component of many joint
custody arrangements, the central issue is not how much
time the child spends with each parent but that the two
parents have equal rights and responsibilities for childrearing. We cannot repeat often enough that joint custody has
been and will probably continue to be defined in numerous
ways. The term joint custody means different things to different people. However, as we will be discussing it in this
book, it is the concept of equal rights and responsibilities
which differentiates joint custody from sole custody. The
legally enforceable equal rights and responsibilities concept
attempts to guarantee that both parents have significant influence upon their child's growth and development.

However, as we have mentioned, custody terms and phrases do not have standard or consistent definitions. There are today numerous terms used to identify custody arrangements with varying legal, moral, and physical rights and responsibilities for childrearing. Terms such as co-parenting, joint parenting, shared custody, divided custody, joint custody, etc., are being used by different people to describe custody arrangements without uniform agreement as to what they mean. Miriam Galper explains that "co-parenting means sharing your children equally," and makes clear that "this is not necessarily a legal agreement, but can be a moral one" (Galper, 1978:16-17). This explanation illustrates the importance of not confusing joint custody with co-parenting, for there is a significant difference between the two. Co-parenting has been practiced by some couples for many years. Following many divorces, both parents attempt to remain active in their children's lives and may attempt to share rights and responsibilities equally. However, in these arrangements legal custody may have been granted to one parent. This means that at that parent's discretion, any one of the agreed upon ways of handling the custody arrangement could be terminated. It also means that in the event of a major disagreement about child rearing, the legal power and control clearly rests with the custodial parent. In joint custody, the legal rights and responsibilities are held in common by both divorced parents. We believe that this is significantly different from an understanding or moral agreement between parents. Much of what has and will be written about joint custody will apply to co-parenting and vice versa. However, the legal difference is paramount and must not be ignored or undervalued. Parents who sincerely want to guarantee themselves the legal rights and responsibilities of sharing in their child's growth and development will want to consider a joint custody agreement. The interest in alternatives to sole custody has resulted in confusion about these key concepts and terms. As more and more states begin to legally define custody options, this confusion and misunderstanding should disappear.

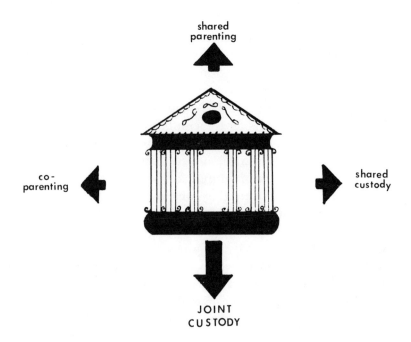

Probably the easiest way to explain the difference between joint custody and sole custody is to consider what happens when one parent is granted sole custody. Let us assume that Bob and Karen Robbins have two children and decide to divorce. They agree between themselves that Karen will have custody of the children. This decision is transmitted by their attorneys to the court, and, as part of the final divorce proceedings, Karen is granted sole custody of the children. Just what does this mean? Simply put, it means that Karen now has control over how the Robbins' children will be raised. Bob has visitation rights, but has forfeited the legally binding right to make decisions which affect his children. As June and William Noble put it, "custody means control. It means ownership, power, authority" (Noble and Noble, 1975:69). Karen can decide both the day-to-day issues such as what the children will wear to school, as well as such important matters as when and where they will seek medical help. She can also decide that the children are too sick to see their father, even when it is his visitation day. Although couples handle custody situations differently, there is no question that the legal responsibility for the child is left with the parent given sole custody. If a major disagreement about childrearing occurs, the only alternative available to the noncustodial parent is his or her ability to persuade the custodial parent or the court. Needless to say, returning to court is a painful, expensive and time-consuming option. Furthermore, it will only be effective if the noncustodial parent can show that the child is being harmed by the other parent.

We have stated that it is the concept of equal rights and responsibility which we believe distinguishes joint custody from other custody arrangements. However, in practice this concept defies a single, all-inclusive definition. There is no single, clear explanation of what equal rights and responsibilities in joint custody actually means. Since this form of custody is a new phenomenon, ways of designing and implementing it are continuously being developed and refined. For example, let us look at two different ways parents within a joint custody arrangement could decide to share their rights and responsibilities about decision making. One method might be called the pure joint custody arrangement. In this type of arrangement, the divorced parents agree to make all major decisions about their children together. In some ways this is similar to what happens in many marriages. Decisions require discussion, bargaining, and accommodations before a decision with which both parents can live can be made. (Later in the book we will address such issues as how to decide what is a major decision, how to facilitate the decision making process, and how to handle situations where parents do not agree.)

A second possible way of handling the equal rights and responsibilities concept involves delineating specific areas in advance—such as health, education, religion, etc.—and deciding which parent will be responsible for making decisions in what area. Obviously there will be a great deal of overlap between specific areas. A way of insuring continuity in decision making and minimizing disagreements will need to be developed in advance if this method is to be successful.

The two methods of implementing joint decision making briefly described above are in reference to major decisions which must be made about the child or children. Our conversations and studies with families involved in joint custody reveal that most day-to-day decisions are made by whichever parent has physical custody of the child at the time. We would not want the reader to think that joint custody means that every time a decision must be made, parents must consult each other. Parents do not call each other every time they must decide whether their child should be allowed to eat a piece of candy or go outside to play. This is clearly *not* the intent or purpose of joint custody. Rather, such custody is a way of insuring that both parents can remain active participants in their child's life by having input into decisions which are likely to have a significant effect on the child's development. Interestingly, when a major decision must be made in sole custody situations, the custodial and noncustodial parent may often discuss the problem and reach a mutual decision. However, in joint custody this is more often the rule, not the informal custom or exception; both parents are insured the legal right to have input into important decisions. Joint custody can reduce the powerlessness —and at times subsequent anger—felt by the parent who in sole custody is denied this right, as well as the pressure and overwhelming responsibility felt by the custodial parent who must often make decisions regarding the children alone.

Although joint custody has recently become an option sought by more and more divorcing parents, it is by no means a totally new idea. For instance, there has been a law in North Carolina since 1953 which permits "divided custody," an arrangement very similar to joint custody. Chapter 50 of the North Carolina Statutes reads:

> An order for custody of a minor child may grant exclusive custody of such child to one person . . . or, if clearly in the best interest of the child, provide for custody in two or more of the same, at such times and for such periods as will in the opinion of the judge, best promote the interests and the welfare of the child. (N.C. Gen. Stat. 13.2)

Although it was not until 1977 that any state had passed a law specifically addressing joint custody, the statutes in California, Iowa, Kansas, Maine, Nevada, North Carolina, Oregon, Texas, and Wisconsin now provide for joint or shared custody arrangements. In October 1977, Oregon passed into law Senate Bill 446. This bill allowed judges to award joint custody, but as Roman and Haddad (1978) point out, it did not encourage the awarding of joint custody, nor did it provide guidelines regarding when it would be appropriate to grant such custody. The pertinent section of the Oregon Bill reads as follows:

> Section 2, ORS 107.105 is amended to read: (1) "Whenever the court grants a decree of annulment or dissolution of marriage or of separation, it has power further to decree as follows: (a) For the future care and custody of the minor children by one party or jointly as it may deem just and proper." (1977 Or. Laws, Ch. 205)

On 1 February 1978 Wisconsin enacted into law a statute expressly providing for joint custody. The Wisconsin law, unlike the Oregon statute, offers a clear and specific definition of joint custody.

(1) (b) The court may give the care and custody of
such children to the parents jointly if the parties so agree
and if the court finds that a joint custody arrangement
would be in the best interests of the child or children.
Joint custody under this paragraph means that both parties
have equal rights and responsibilities to the minor child
and neither party's rights are superior (Wis. Stat. 242.24)

However, it was not until California's law went into effect
on January 1, 1980, that a state statute clearly encouraged
joint custody. The opening statement of the California law
explains:

Section 1. Section 4600. The Legislature finds and de-
clares that it is the public policy of this state to assure
minor children of frequent and continuing contact with
both parents after the parents have separated or dissolved
their marriage, and in order to effect such policy, it is
necessary to encourage parents to share the rights and responsibilities of child rearing.

The law appears to favor an award of joint custody when
both or either parent requests it. If a judge does not award
such custody, reasons for denial must be stated in the decision. Interestingly, even if sole custody is granted "the court
shall consider which parent is more likely to allow the child
frequent and continuing contact with the noncustodial
parent. . . ."

Although a growing number of states have laws concerning joint custody, this does not mean that parents in
these states can expect to be awarded such a custody arrangement merely upon request. The awarding of any type of
custody can be a lengthy and confusing process. The joint
custody provision in most state statutes does not propose to
hasten or simplify this process. What it does, we believe, is
to recognize joint custody as a legitimate custody option. The
law also begins to delineate some of the major provisions
inherent in joint custody. One of the drafters of the Wisconsin law, believes that its language establishes joint cus-

tody as a legal concept independent of the child's physical placement. Whatever legal powers custody connotes are now held by both parents jointly (Bondehagen, 1977). As we have said previously, the crucial difference between sole custody and joint custody is the concept of equal rights and responsibilities, not the physical whereabouts of the child.

CASE LAW

Although joint custody has been enacted into law only in the states previously mentioned, it does not appear to be illegal in any state. Courts in some states have permitted joint custody type arrangements, even though the state lacks a joint custody statute. Basically this means that these courts have interpreted existing state custody laws to allow for joint custody. Therefore, one should not think that because a given state does not have a specific provision for joint custody this eliminates such an option from consideration. It appears that if it so desires any state court can award joint custody. We will discuss several interesting cases in which the courts have either agreed or refused to award this type of custody.

Often a joint custody arrangement has been awarded when the courts believed that one or more of the following criteria were met: first, both parents were fit; second, the court felt that joint custody would lessen the trauma of divorce for the child and the parents; third, and most important, joint custody was felt to be in the child's best interests. Some courts have boldly asserted that joint custody is indeed in the best interests of the child or children. The New York Supreme Court, Queens Division, expressed this belief in the 1974 case of *Perroti* v. *Perroti,* stating

> the trauma that flows from the dissolution of the marriage should be prevented whenever possible to the extent that the court must be ever vigilant in insulating the infants from injury resulting from such trauma. This can be accomplished by providing maximum accessibility as between parent and child. In this regard, the history of mari-

tal disputes has been fraught with the spawning of "needless round(s) of tension and conflict until 'death do them part' ...." As such, many children have been innocent dupes and victims of those parents who have used their custodial rights as bargaining agents and instruments of intimidation in seeking an unfair advantage over the other parent. Therefore, where joint custody could properly be employed, would it not serve to remove the psychological "abrasiveness" that one parent may utilize as against the other?

Moreover, common sense and experience suggest that the traumatic upheavals brought about by a "broken home" are difficult enough for young children, even older ones, to understand and accept. By contrast the concept of "joint custody" can serve to give that measure of psychological support and uplift to each parent which would communicate itself to the children in measures of mutual love, mutual attention and mutual training. The string of security and stability that would flow from mother to child to father, with "joint custody" serving as the emotional fulcrum, would but strengthen the parent-child unit in what otherwise could be a completely destroyed marital home. ... (Perroti v. Perroti)

New York appears to have had the most case experience with joint custody. In the New York case of Levy v. Levy, the court awarded joint custody of a thirteen-year-old boy to his divorcing parents. The judge interviewed the boy privately and found him to be mature and insightful. He ordered that the parents would have joint custody, but stipulated that the boy was to live with his mother for two years, after which time he could decide with which parent he wanted to reside. The judge concluded that,

the court grants each parent joint control of the child's education and upbringing and reasons that by granting the parents an equal voice in the raising of their child much of the acrimony and ill will generated by the divorce will be ameliorated. Joint custody will also serve to give the measure of psychological support and uplift to each parent which would communicate itself to the child in measure of mutual love, mutual attention and mutual training. (*Levy* v. *Levy*)

In *Krois* v. *Krois,* the court awarded the couple joint custody with physical custody of the couple's two children to be "with the father in the established marital residence." The court went on to add, "Where children are not of tender years ... case law presents no legal impediment to joint custody where both parents are fit and the award would be in the best interest of the child" (*Krois* v. *Krois*).

While New York has had the most experience with joint custody, other states should be mentioned in an historical overview of such custody awards. A 1962 Missouri case, a 1956 case in California, and a 1948 Virginia case all involve joint custody type decisions. The Virginia case, though more than thirty years old, echoes many of the concerns voiced by those who are requesting joint custody today. The court concluded as follows:

> The advisability of dividing the custody of the child has been seriously considered. While there are certain disadvantages in such division, there are also important advantages and benefits. It gives the child the experience of two separate homes. The child is entitled to the love, advice, and training of both her father and her mother. Frequent association, contact, and friendly relations with both of her parents will protect her future welfare if one of her parents should die. It gives recognition to the rights of parents who have performed obligation as parents. (*Mullen* v. *Mullen*)

These cases are, of course, only a small sample of instances in which joint custody has been awarded. Most joint custody decisions are the result of negotiations between the couple's attorney (s) and the judge; consequently, they receive little attention. The cases described here serve to exemplify the philosophy of some members of the judicial system in regard to the benefits which children may derive from joint custody.

However, not all courts agree that joint custody type arrangements are preferable to sole custody awards. Some state

courts have refused or overturned joint custody or similar
types of custody awards, believing that they are in general
not in the child's best interests. In some of the cases cited
below, the courts overturned custody decisions in which the
parents were awarded shared physical custody of their children. Although these cases are not pure joint custody situations by our definition, they do contain enough similarities
to help us understand why some courts do not favor joint
custody.

In a 1976 Washington, D.C. case, the District of Columbia
Court of Appeals reversed a trial court's order granting custody of a child to its mother for two months and then to its
father for one month on a continuous basis. The court decided that "without a showing of any exceptional circumstances or a compelling reason why such a custody arrangement would promote the best interest of the child, such an
arrangement is in error." (*Utley* v. *Utley*)

Following a mother's appeal, the Vermont Supreme Court
also overturned a joint custody award. Like the case cited
above, the court held that unless there are special circumstances, joint custody should not be granted. The court explained that in its opinion joint custody "gives rise to special
problems." The court also stated:

> Problems arising from the lack of a stable home life and
> frequent changes of habit also may be expected to arise
> more frequently in joint custody than in sole custody
> cases. This is so for two reasons. The first is that in the
> sole custody situation, the child generally spends more
> time with the custodial parent than with the visiting
> parent, thus establishing a dominant routine. The second
> has to do with the problem of cooperation discussed above.
> Where parents maintain separate households and differing
> routines, perhaps even different notions of acceptable be-
> havior and discipline, the likelihood of confusing the chil-
> dren is increased where neither parent has the final word.
> (*Lumbra* v. *Lumbra*)

A Florida case, *Gall* v. *Gall*, is another example of a joint
custody award being overturned. Apparently when the trial

court awarded joint custody, it also allowed the fourteen-year-old girl to decide with which parent she would like to live. This ambiguity seems to be the reason the award was overturned and the case was remanded with instruction to award custody of the child to one parent or the other.

In 1966, the St. Louis, Missouri, Court of Appeals overturned a joint custody type arrangement where the custody of the child changed from one parent to the other each year. The court stated:

> Generally, except for good reason, a child of divorced parents should not be shifted periodically from one home to another since in most instances the interest of the child is best served from a standpoint of stability if one or the other parent is given full custody with reasonable visitation rights to the other parent. (*Wood* v. *Wood*)

These refused or overturned joint custody type decisions have certain similarities. First, several of the cases were appealed by one of the parents. This may suggest that either the parents did not initially agree on joint custody or else were later dissatisfied with the arrangement. Second, the overturned cases in general did not carefully explain why the arrangement was initially granted, how it was to serve the child's best interests. Third, the courts in these cases did not look favorably upon the child alternatively living with each parent. These similarities suggest that the court was more likely to deny joint custody in cases where it was not well conceived or where both parents were not in agreement.

Even a brief review of case law demonstrates that there have been joint custody type arrangements in the United States for years. However, this custody option has received little attention or examination. The lack of awareness and understanding of joint custody has been evident not only in the general public, but also in the legal sector and other professions who work with families in the process of divorce. Consequently, joint custody is not frequently requested nor suggested as an alternative to traditional custody decisions. Some persons who have heard about it react with confusion or discomfort because it is new and different. A striking example of this occurred at the August 1975 American Bar Association annual meeting. During a session of the family law section, Doris Sassower urged that courts consider awarding joint custody of children to divorcing parents:

> Ms. Sassower stressed that what many fathers now want is not just extended visitation but true parental rights: i.e., an equal voice in decisions affecting the child's future. She was immediately attacked by numerous male members of the panel and audience who unequivocally declared that (1) any father who says he wants extended visitation or continual parental rights is a liar, who is merely seeking to harass the wife in order to pry into her new social life and exert pressure that will force down her monetary demands, and (2) that any attorney who argues such a position is irresponsively focusing on the parents' opposing rights and ignoring the best interest of the child's since everyone knows that shuttling back and forth is bad for a child's well-being, and (3) that anyone who obtains an order for joint custody has merely proved that the judge was too soft hearted and opposing counsel was untalented. (1 Fam. L. Rep. 2708)

Fortunately, not all criticism of joint custody is so callous or unfounded. Many who are familiar with the concept raise serious questions about the effects joint custody will have on divorcing families. These are important questions which need to be discussed and answered. As people begin to discuss joint custody openly, a more in-depth analysis and study of this custody alternative will be possible. Later, as we examine joint custody in detail, we will also be forced to look at how custody decisions in general are made. Such an inspection may well uncover a pattern with little rhyme or reason, where a decision at times causes more problems than it solves. By writing about joint custody before it becomes an option practiced by many people, we hope to offer guidelines which will prevent the kind of problems that have resulted from custody decision making to date.

We wish to conclude this chapter as it began, asking the question, "What is joint custody?" We have seen that it is an idea, an option, and a loosely-defined concept. We have defined it as a legal agreement made at the time of divorce which permits both parents to remain active in their child's life by sharing rights and responsibilities related to child-rearing. Couples can design joint custody agreements to meet their family's specific needs; they are not bound by highly standardized rules and regulations. Of course, their agreement must be accepted by the courts; but, increasingly, there is reason to believe that a well-conceived agreement taking into account the important idiosyncrasies of a divorcing family will be looked upon favorably. After all, the court is interested in granting a custody decision that will help parents provide a healthy emotional and physical environment for the children involved. Later in this book we will offer specific suggestions about what to include in a joint custody agreement. For now, we urge the reader to think of it as an arrangment that:

1. meets the emotional and physical needs of both children and parents;
2. allows both parents to remain active participants in their children's lives;
3. permits enough flexibility for the family to constructively plan a custody arrangement based on its specific needs; and
4. thoroughly avoids the "I win, you lose" notion all too common in the process and outcome of custody decision making.

The concept of a joint custody arrangement that can accomplish these objectives is as challenging as it is exciting. It will demand a great deal of work on the part of all involved to make such an arrangement succeed. We believe the potential payoff for some families easily justifies the time and effort expended.

4

The Effects of Divorce on Children

The United States is experiencing a dramatic increase in both the number of divorces and the number of children involved in divorce. In 1976 the 1,077,000 divorces directly affected over one million children. Today one out of six children in the United States is involved in divorce (United States Vital Statistics Report, 1977). It has been estimated that 7 million children under the age of eighteen live in "single-parent" families (Klebanow, 1976). Divorce and subsequent sole custody of children is a major reason why an increasing number of children and adults are living in nontraditional family units.

In this chapter we will examine the effects of divorce on children, perhaps the most vulnerable members of families. This information should be useful and interesting to parents in the midst of divorce and professionals who work with such families. We will be utilizing this information in the next chapter to show how joint custody can prevent or at least minimize some of the adverse effects divorce may have on children.

Although all children react uniquely to their parents' separation or divorce, a number of factors contribute to how

divorce may affect children. The most important factors include the child's age, sex, intellectual and emotional development, and the environment and familial milieu before and
following the divorce. At times, the reactions of children to
their parents' divorce may seem overwhelming to all family
members. Couples who are considering divorce may receive
criticism from their friends and relatives who ask, "How can
you do this to your children?" Sometimes it is one of the
parents, upon realizing that the other is considering divorce,
who asks the same question.

However, despite the difficulties divorce causes for the
entire family, many authorities believe that it is more advantageous for a child to live in a single-parent family than to
remain in a traditional nuclear family where there is discord
(Anthony, 1974; Despert, 1962; Gardner, 1970; Roberts and
Roberts, 1974). Gardner tells us that "the child living with
unhappy married parents more often gets into psychiatric
difficulty than the one whose mismatched parents have been
healthy and strong enough to sever their troubled relationship" (Gardner, 1970:xix).

Perhaps the question "How can you do this to your children?" is more appropriately asked of parents who raise their
children in a family where tension and hostility are constantly present. In a recent study, Deborah A. Luepnitz
(1979) interviewed college students regarding their parents'
divorces. All of the students interviewed had experienced
parental divorce before the age of sixteen. This investigator
found that the young people reported most frequently that
marital conflict which preceded the divorce was the most
difficult phase of the divorce process.

A considerable amount of research has examined the effects of divorce on children. Some of it has studied the divorce process and its specific effects on children of all ages,
while other research has looked at how children of different
age groups react to divorce. The reader should bear in mind
that although this research has certainly contributed to a

greater understanding of divorce and its impact on children, it is by no means complete or conclusive. In some instances we have included studies which have reached different conclusions about the same issue. This was done to demonstrate that disagreement and debate does exist regarding the effects of divorce on children. In spite of this contradictory data, we believe that a review of this literature will help the reader to more fully understand the area of divorce and children.

THE DIVORCE PROCESS

Divorce is often viewed as a process rather than as a single event. Most children of an unhappy marriage experience its effects well before a divorce actually occurs. Frequently the children are involved in the disagreements or conflicts between parents. Some children may begin to side, or feel pressure to side, with one parent or the other long before the divorce itself. The sections that follow briefly discuss some of the effects the process of divorce may have on children.

Crisis

When children are confronted with the reality of their parents' divorce, a crisis may result (Anthony, 1974; Sugar, 1970a, 1970b). A crisis occurs "when a person faces an obstacle to important life goals that is, for a time, insurmountable through the utilization of customary methods of problem-solving" (Caplan, 1951:18).

Like adults, children are normally in a state of emotional equilibrium or balance (Aguilera and Messick, 1974). When a problem becomes overwhelming, the balance is destroyed. If this occurs, tension increases as the child uses his or her normal problem-solving techniques to deal with the situation. Usually the increased tension will cause the child to mobilize internal resources and seek external ones. If the child is unable to either solve the problem or adapt, there may be significant emotional upset and disorganization.

Signs of anxiety, fear, depression, and helplessness are emo-

tional clues that signify the potential for crisis. Sleep difficulties, change in eating habits, physical complaints, and
behavior problems are other warning signals that the child
is experiencing significant difficulties with his or her parents'
divorce. Most children will experience some of these symptoms, since divorce is likely to be a very stressful experience.
When crisis symptoms are especially pronounced, or when
they last for an extended period of time, a child may need
professional assistance. If professional intervention is necessary, the goal will be to return the child to a level of emotional equilibrium which is the same or healthier than his
or her precrisis state.

Grief

A predominate feeling experienced by children during
their parents' divorce is grief. The feeling of grief is often
associated with guilt (Anthony, 1974; Derdeyn, 1977; Sugar,
1970b) .

Since separation and divorce typically leads to one parents'
departure from the home, the feeling of grief may initially
stem from this perceived physical loss. Grieving may be
associated with feelings of guilt because children may won-

der if they are the cause of their parents' divorce. As time
passes, the lack of day-to-day involvement with the departed
parent may increase the child's feeling of grief. Younger children are especially prone to separation anxiety, a fear which
develops in response to parental absence. The grieving that
children may experience during and after divorce is similar
to the grief reaction following the death of a loved one.

Shame and Resentment

Some children feel ashamed and resentful following their
parents' divorce (Anthony, 1974; Wallerstein and Kelly,
1974). Lacking a satisfactory explanation or understanding
of why the divorce occurred, the child may feel responsible.
Some children may be ashamed or embarrassed that their
parents are divorcing and may view themselves as failures
(Wallerstein and Kelly, 1974).

Resentment or anger is also a common feeling following
the divorce (Anthony, 1974; Gardner, 1970; Wallerstein and
Kelly, 1974). This occurs when the child's wishes that the
parents reunite are frustrated. As children begin to recognize
that their parents will not remain together despite their
wishes, they are forced to deal with the subsequent situation.
Postdivorce changes, such as the lack of day-to-day contact
with father, having a mother working, or having a parent
dating may all be met with confusion, anger, or resentment.
These hostile feelings may be directed outward toward either
parent, toward relatives, or toward friends—or they may be
internalized by the child.

Negative Perceptions of Future Relationships

Some authorities believe that a long-term effect of divorce
on children relates to their future perceptions of relationships and marriage (Anthony, 1974; Sorosky, 1977; Wallerstein and Kelly, 1974). Some children of divorced parents
contend that they will never marry. This feeling may arise

from children generalizing negative perceptions of their parents' marriage to all marriages.

Children who have experienced the effects of their parents' unhappy marriages and subsequent divorces may as adults be leary of committing themselves to marital or similar relationships. There is also the possibility that children may in later years repeat behaviors and interactions learned from their parents and may recreate in their own marriage similar difficulties and problems.

Stigma

Society may present special problems to a child of divorced parents. Although a fairly large percentage of children live with only one parent, the "single-parent" family is still viewed as different, or even as deviant. A stigma continues to be attached to such a family (Brandwein, Brown, and Fox, 1974; Horowitz and Perdue, 1977; Kessler, 1975).

Gardner points out that many children whose parents are divorced experience problems relating to children from two-parent homes; other children are often hostile or demeaning to a child whose parents are separated or divorced. Gardner claims that this problem stems in part from parents who continue to have prejudiced ideas about divorce and who pass on these prejudices to their children; some children have no difficulty interacting with other children, but feel bad about their parents' divorce because they view themselves as unlike other children (Gardner, 1970). It is often difficult for children of divorced parents to recognize that many of their peers are much the same as they. This can cause children to isolate themselves at a time when social contact and support is especially important.

Depression, Aggression, and Antisocial Behavior

Some researchers have linked depression, aggression, and antisocial behavior of children with divorce. These conclusions have resulted from examining the effects of parental absence—a phrase referring to the loss or perceived loss of a parent due to illness, death, desertion, separation, divorce, foster home placement, etc.

There are several factors, however, which make it necessary to question the relevance of some of these studies to divorce. First, several of them examined paternal absence due to a number of reasons such as death, desertion, divorce, and separation; this makes it very difficult to know whether the effects of the absence studied are related to one, more than one, or all of these reasons. Second, the studies do not clearly state what parental absence means; for instance, they do not specify whether the child has some contact with the absent parent (as is likely in divorce) or whether the child never sees the absent parent (as is the case in death and desertion).

In spite of the above-mentioned limitations, these studies are often quoted and discussed when the effects of divorce on children are debated. Consequently, a person who wants to become well-informed about divorce and children should be aware of their merits and drawbacks.

Aggression in children five to ten years of age—in the form of acting out problems—has been linked to parental separation and divorce (Felner, Stohlberg and Cowen, 1975). These researchers have studied referral patterns to a school mental health program and concluded that divorce can contribute to behavior problems at school. Other studies (Anderson, 1968; Douglas, 1970) have shown that a relationship exists in boys between antisocial behavior or delinquency and paternal absence. Absence of the father has been found to be particularly important when boys are between four and seven years of age (Anderson, 1968). However, other findings (Rutter, 1971) suggest that antisocial behavior is associated with the quality of the parents' marriage, rather than with the separation between parent and child. Rutter contends that delinquency is associated with separations which follow parental discord or conflict. The results of his research suggest that children are adversely affected by disharmony and tension in the home, but not by the actual breakup of the family. These contradictory findings demonstrate that there is considerable debate about the correlation between antisocial behavior in boys and paternal absence.

Researchers have also linked depression in childhood with parental loss (Caplan and Douglas, 1969; McDermott, 1970). The results of these studies support the theory that a relationship exists between parental deprivation and depression. In the Caplan and Douglas (1969) study, broken homes— whether due to divorce, desertion, or illness—were considered together making it impossible to accurately weigh these findings as they specifically relate to divorce. McDermott's research (1970) studied children in a psychiatric hospital; consequently, his results should not be generalized to all children of divorce. However, the children studied did show depressive symptomatology as well as problems with identification: "Usually there was an unconscious conspiracy of both mother and child, sometimes one more than the other, to recreate the lost father through the child's identification with his traits" (McDermott, 1970:425).

Contrary findings are presented by James R. Morrison (1974). Also sampling psychiatrically hospitalized children, Morrison did not find that depression occurred more frequently among children of divorced parents. His results suggest that there is no relationship between the parents' marital status and the child's symptomatology. Once again, we find contradictory results, thus leaving open the question of whether or not divorce is a contributing factor to depression in children.

Although it is helpful to examine the divorce process in its entirety as we have done above, it is also important to understand how divorce may affect children at different stages in their development. The following section will highlight the effects of divorce on young children, school-age children, and adolescents.

Effects of Divorce on Young Children

Divorce frequently occurs when the children in the family are young (Derdeyn, 1977). A good deal of research has examined the effects of divorce on children from birth to six years of age.

From a developmental standpoint, a young child from birth to age two is struggling with a conflict basic to his or her ability to exist in this environment. The child is attempting to gain an internal sense of trust and autonomy, rather than that of mistrust and doubt (Erikson, 1963). According to Erik Erikson, a well-known authority in the area of child development, these are the first developmental conflicts that a child is faced with in the movement toward maturity.

Research has shown that the development of trust and autonomy is hindered by the absence of the father in the family (Santrock, 1970). Children whose fathers were absent due to divorce, desertion, or separation demonstrated less basic trust and autonomy in their environment than a similar group of boys whose fathers were present. This same researcher, John W. Santrock, also explored the effect of father absence on the cognitive or intellectual development of young children compared to older children (Santrock, 1972). Early absence of the father, when the child is zero to five years old, was found to be more detrimental than later absence of the father, when the child is six to eleven years old. Father-absent children scored lower than father-present children on cognitive measures such as IQ and achievement tests. Interestingly, the effects of father absence on cognitive scores were more pronounced for boys than for girls. This may suggest that in terms of cognitive development, absence of the same-sex parent is more significant than absence of the opposite-sex parent for children of this particular age. However, an important factor which must be considered when evaluating the significance of these findings is that the sample under study included more children of deserted fathers, a situation which may be more detrimental than either divorce or separation.

Another very important developmental task for the young child is that of gender identification (Fraiberg, 1959). Identification is a process which involves incorporating qualities of another individual into one's own personality. In gender identification, the child begins to model, or take on, qualities or characteristics of the same-sex parent. By the age of six, most children have come to accept and be content with the fact that they are either male or female (Fraiberg, 1959). Without appropriate male and female role models, gender identification is more difficult to achieve. In divorced families where one parent has minimal involvement with the child, it is possible that the child's gender identification may be hindered (Westman, 1972).

The egocentric or self-centered nature of young children (Flavell, 1963) also contributes to how they view the process of divorce. Young children tend to view the world as revolving around themselves. Wishes are synonymous with reality. Consequently, when a young child's wish for his parents to remain together is frustrated, a very difficult period ensues. For instance, the child may perceive the departure of one parent as a rejection of him or her personally (Westman, 1972). Furthermore, egocentricity contributes to a child's continual wish and belief that its parents will remarry even when presented with contradictory information. Because young children regard everything in relation to themselves, they may believe they are the cause of their parents' divorce. Children often believe that one parent left the home because of them. As one would expect, the younger the child, the less ability he or she has to form a realistic perspective on the divorce experience.

Perhaps the most thorough and conclusive research regarding the effects of divorce on children has been done by Judith Wallerstein and Joan Kelly in northern California. They observed the impact of divorce on each family member shortly after the parents' separation and again one year later. Their reports provide a relatively complete picture of the divorce process and its effect on children at various ages.

The first of these examines the effects of divorce on preschool children (Wallerstein and Kelly, 1975). From their study of thirty-four children, these investigators identified distinguishable responses among preschoolers of different ages. For instance, children two and one-half to three and one-fourth years of age showed significant changes in behavior, such as crying, fearfulness, regressions in toilet training, sleep problems, tantrums, etc. "The most enduring symptom was that of pervasive neediness" (Wallerstein and Kelly, 1975:615). For children ages three and three-fourths to four and one-fourth years, family disruption appeared to have a detrimental effect on their developing self-image and esteem. Children 5 to 6 years of age were better able to understand divorce and its associated changes. Their reactions to parental separation and divorce were manifested in forms of heightened anxiety and aggression, such as restlessness, moodiness, irritability, and temper tantrums.

EFFECTS OF DIVORCE ON SCHOOL-AGE CHILDREN

Divorce also poses special problems for a school-age child. Although children seven to twelve years of age may experience the same feelings and thoughts as a younger child, they are usually more capable of understanding issues related to the divorce.

One of Kelly and Wallerstein's reports (1976) focuses on the effects of divorce on children seven and eight years old. They cite parental absence as being very difficult for the child of this age:

> The child frequently perceives the parent's departure as a departure from him personally.... In this respect, the central event of divorce for children is psychologically comparable to the event of death, and frequently evokes

similar responses of disbelief, shock and denial. (Wallerstein and Kelly, 1976:22)

Boys especially showed a strong sense of loss after the father left the home. According to Wallerstein and Kelly, the most striking response to parental separation for children seven and eight years old was sadness. Unfortunately, none of the children interviewed perceived the post-divorce visiting situation as adequately compensating for the loss of the noncustodial parent. The children who were reasonably satisfied with the visiting situation were those seeing the noncustodial parent several times a week.

These researchers also discuss the effects of divorce on thirty-one children between nine and ten years of age (Wallerstein and Kelly, 1976). The children of this age group also experienced a great sense of loss and loneliness as a result of their parents' divorce. The loneliness was characterized by the child's feeling of having to side with one parent or the other in what the child perceived as a battle:

> Thus, paralyzed by their own conflicting loyalties and the severe psychic or real penalties which attach to choice, many children refrained from choice and felt alone and desolate, with no place to turn for comfort or parenting. (Wallerstein and Kelly, 1976:425)

Children seven to twelve years old are very involved in tasks related to school. There is an increasing need to produce, achieve, and learn. Erik Erikson has termed this the stage of industry versus inferiority (1963). The child attempts to ward off inferiority by accomplishing tasks which it perceives will lead to success. Children of this age typically work hard to avoid a sense of failure. In spite of this desire to achieve, feelings of confusion, loneliness, and anger experienced during a divorce process may lead to a decline in school performance (Anthony, 1974; Felner et al., 1975; Wallerstein and Kelly, 1976; Westman, 1972). For some children this can be devastating. Such a decline can damage the child's self-esteem, which is now more dependent than ever on how the child stands in relation to his or her peers. Friends and peers are significant influences in children's lives at this age, and anything which is perceived as a major threat to their relationships with these significant others may cause problems.

EFFECTS OF DIVORCE ON ADOLESCENTS

Several investigators have explored the effects of divorce on adolescents (Sorosky, 1977; Wallerstein and Kelly, 1974; Westman, 1972). Unquestionably, more research is needed regarding this age group.

In contrast to young or school-age children, adolescents do not usually perceive parental divorce as happening to them personally. The adolescent is better able to analyze the situation. Unlike other age groups, they may realize and acknowledge that there are possible benefits related to their parents' divorce.

An adolescent is struggling with several developmental tasks crucial to their ability to succeed with the adjustment to adulthood. One of these is answering the question, "Who am I?" and developing a sense of identity (Erikson, 1963). Adolescents achieve this in part by using their parents as role models. The same-sex parent is very important in this process. In most divorces, contact with one parent is significantly diminished; this decreases the opportunity for parent-child interaction and may interfere with the adolescent's ability to develop a well-integrated sense of identity.

The adolescent is also attempting to further individuate himself from the family. In the process of gaining independence, this detachment or separation from the family is necessary. Dependency-independency conflicts are common at this age. At times, adolescents seek freedom and rebel against authority; at other times they do not trust their own sense of emerging maturity and covertly seek guidelines from adults.

Divorce may interfere with the parental support and advice so needed in adolescence. Teenagers are confronted with many important decisions, some of which have lifelong consequences. Choices about one's career, education, intimate relationships, and lifestyle are among the myriad issues facing an adolescent. Parents in the midst of divorce may be so preoccupied with their own problems that they are unable to provide the day-to-day guidance an adolescent requires in order to successfully cope with the move toward adulthood (Sorosky, 1977).

Wallerstein and Kelly (1974) studied a group of twenty-one adolescents thirteen years of age and older whose parents had divorced. These adolescents felt angry, sad, and betrayed by their parents' divorce. Some of them experienced loyalty conflicts which resulted in resentment toward both parents. Interestingly, adolescents who withdrew or distanced themselves from the family situation during the divorce process showed increased maturity and capacity for positive regard for at least one parent one year after the divorce. This suggests that an adolescent's emotional detachment at the time of divorce may be an adaptive mechanism which contributes to a continuation of normal development.

SUMMARY

We have attempted to provide the reader with an overview of the effects of divorce on children. In general, the research is inconclusive and suffers from numerous methodological limitations. However, it does suggest that, like their parents, children experience short-term adverse effects such as grief, loneliness, anger, and feelings of rejection in response to divorce. Whether or not divorce leads to significant long-term problems such as gender identification confusion, depression, antisocial behavior, and difficulty in future interpersonal relationships is debatable.

Divorce is often a very difficult experience for children. Many of their problems are related to the perceived loss of one parent typically resulting from sole custody arrangements after divorce. For this reason, it is imperative that we seriously consider whether other custody arrangements can alleviate or minimize the potential adverse effects of divorce on children. Drawing on the research previously discussed, chapter 5 will begin by exploring how for some divorcing families a joint custody arrangement may provide advantages for children which would not exist with sole custody.

5

Joint Custody: Its Benefits and Drawbacks

Joint custody may be a preferable option for some divorcing families. Although such an arrangement offers advantages to children and parents which do not exist with sole custody, it also has its limitations and potential problems. Only after weighing both the potential benefits and the potential drawbacks can a divorcing family decide if joint custody is an option worth pursuing.

POTENTIAL BENEFITS FOR CHILDREN AND PARENTS

Many of the effects of divorce on children are related to the absence of one parent. The noncustodial mother or father may become more like a visitor than a true parent and often has much less contact than previously with the child and little opportunity for offering input into the child's day-to-day upbringing. In this way divorce can drastically change the parent-child relationship. The infrequent visitation privileges typically allotted a noncustodial parent are rarely adequate to compensate for his or her absence, and some children may perceive the infrequency as proof of further rejection. For many children this postdivorce situation is quite difficult and painful.

A joint custody arrangement may be able to prevent or at least diminish some of the undesirable feelings experienced by children following their parents' divorce. Obviously, it will not make the divorce experience completely stress-free, but it may provide advantages to children which they would not have under a sole custody arrangement.

Joint custody recognizes that both parents have a right and desire to be involved in their child's life. In effect, it says to a child, "You still have two parents." The fact that both still love and care about their child is communicated in several ways in a joint custody arrangement. Both parents remain active participants in their child's upbringing through their input into decisions which have a major effect on the child's life, and the child knows that both parents are available to give advice and guidance. In arrangements where the child's physical custody is shared, the child will of course continue to see both parents regularly. A fourteen-year-old girl who had been living in a joint custody arrangement for six years explained: "I feel closer to my parents. I have friends who are with their fathers or mothers only one or two days a week, and compared to that, I like our arrangement better" (Kellogg, 1977:56).

While in some sole custody arrangements the active involvement of both parents continues, joint custody maximizes the possibility that this will occur. Such involvement may alleviate or at least minimize those feelings of loss, sadness, guilt, and anger which children often experience as a result of their parents' divorce. Dana, an eight-year-old, said that she "was a little bit scared" when her parents divorced. However, despite this, she feels positively about joint custody. "I think it's wonderful! . . . I can walk to school from my mom *and* my dad's house! . . . I want to be with both my mom and dad, so it's good" (Ware, 1979:51).

We discussed earlier how parental absence has been linked to antisocial behavior or delinquency in boys and to depression in children, noting that there are conflicting findings

and problems in generalizing some of the results to divorce situations only. However, joint custody can have the potential to prevent such problems by allowing the child to have continued contact with both parents.

Continued contact with parents may also prevent problems related to gender identification. Michael Lamb explains: "From the studies reviewed thus far it seems that we can state only that an affectionate father-child relationship appears to facilitate the sex-role development of the children"

(Lamb, 1976:15) . Joint custody has a greater potential than sole custody to provide a child with appropriate gender role models. This involvement with both male and female models is important to the child's developing sense of identity.

Children often experience loyalty conflicts, even while their parents are married. When a separation or divorce occurs, these conflicts may cause problems; we described how children feel that they must make a choice between their two parents. In contested custody cases, a child may be asked directly to state with whom he or she wants to live, especially if the child is older. A child who feels that he or she must make a choice and side with one parent or the other is usually in a "no win" situation. Assuming that the relationship with both parents is good, it is unrealistic to expect a child to remain untroubled by the consequences of such a decision. Parents may intentionally or unintentionally contribute to this dilemma. Both a custodial parent who asks, "Aren't you happy you live with me?" and a noncustodial parent who inquires, "Wouldn't you rather stay with me?" are further pressuring their child to choose one parent over the other.

Joint custody removes the feeling that a child needs to make such a choice. This option respects the child's positive relationships with both parents. When Ted and Jill Simons told their children about their divorce, they also reassured them that they would not be forced to choose one parent or the other. Jill Simons explains: "We're *both* good parents and we've always been with our kids, and besides, we promised them they wouldn't have to choose" (Ware, 1979:44) .

Joint custody may also decrease some of the stigma which still surrounds divorce. Children from divorced families often feel different from their friends from traditional, two-parent homes. A second grader who is asked in a school discussion, "What time does your daddy come home?" may be embarrassed and ashamed that Daddy no longer lives at home. Although joint custody doesn't change the reality that the parents are divorced, it does maintain characteristics of the nuclear family to a greater degree than does sole custody in that children are still very much aware that they have two parents. This awareness may be reinforced by friends and relatives who understand joint custody. When we asked a joint custody father about the reactions of his friends and relatives he said, "They think it's terrific! They recognize that my relationship with my son is growing, and that I wanted to spend more time with him. This I'm sure gets communicated to my son."

A child who lives in a sole custody arrangement may have limited exposure to varying opinions, lifestyles, and role models. A custodial parent has primary responsibility for the child's total physical, emotional, educational, and religious upbringing. In the case of a younger child, the custodial parent may be the only role model from which the child can learn. In any case, custodial parents have both control and responsibility over who and what will influence their child's life, while parents who have joint custody share this huge responsibility. The greater exposure to different beliefs and lifestyles experienced in such arrangements can enhance a child's growth and development. Continued contact with both parents can offer a wider repertoire of behaviors, skills, and ideas from which youngsters may choose. One joint custody father explained that his daughter may gain some sense of independence from both he and his former wife's different lifestyles, values, and beliefs: "When she gets older she'll be in a better position to choose how she wants to live her life."

Finally, joint custody may reduce the possibility that the child will in the future view male-female relationships negatively. We described how children who experience turmoil and hostility before, during, and after a divorce may generalize their negative feelings to future relationships, causing many to insist that they will never marry (Sorosky, 1977). Obviously, joint custody cannot obliterate what occurred before the divorce; however, children are more likely to have a positive attitude about marriage when their parents are amiable and respectful towards each other during and following a divorce. By minimizing the potential for custody disputes and requiring the parents to work together, joint custody can promote these positive feelings.

Perhaps the most positive aspect of joint custody for parents is the alleviation of the great sense of loss experienced by many noncustodial mothers and fathers. In a joint custody arrangement, both parents are seen as fit, responsible adults, who love and have something positive to offer their children. No longer is one parent relegated to a visitor role, dependent upon the other's good will for any significant input into the child's development. The concept of shared rights and responsibilities central to a joint custody arrangement is an attempt to ensure that neither parent feels that he or she has lost their child following divorce. Anne, in reflecting on her husband's desire to share custody of their child, explained: "He loves his daughter, and wants to be a 'real father.' I feel really strongly about joint custody. I've met many men who are fathers without children. Sure, they have visiting rights but it isn't the same. They're not full participants—some of them become court jesters. They think, 'How shall I entertain my child this weekend?' Entertaining isn't really what parenting is all about."

Joint custody may actually enhance the relationship between divorcing parents. A custody fight—potentially the most traumatic aspect of divorce—is avoided, and childrearing remains a mutual task which necessitates cooperation, communication, and respect. Conflict may be reduced because neither individual is threatened by the loss of the child; rather the parenting needs of both mother and father continue to be satisfied. A recent study based on interviews with 127 divorced Boston fathers compared their satisfaction in four different types of custody situations: (1) full-time or full-custody fathers; (2) half-time or joint custody fathers; (3) quarter-time fathers; and (4) occasional fathers (Dullea,

1978). Through direct interviews, the investigators determined that the ideal custody arrangement appears to be one in which the two parents agreed to share custody equally. In addition, the half-time father had "the lowest level of conflict with his former mate as well as the most positive attitude about becoming a father again" (Dullea, 1978:6).

Parents in joint custody arrangements also benefit from sharing the serious responsibility of childrearing rather than shouldering it alone. In a divorce study by Brown, *et al.* (1976), the authors found that ⅔ of the Boston-area women interviewed expressed concern about the increased responsibility of single parenthood. Raising children is a difficult process for two parents; when one parent must handle childrearing alone, it can seem overwhelming. It may be an especially awesome task when a parent has been accustomed to sharing such responsibilities.

Joint custody can provide a sense of psychological comfort, since both parents know that important decisions will not be made alone. It can also provide pragmatic comfort, since both realize that there is a co-provider, should a crisis or other unforeseen situation arise.

In many cases, joint custody provides both parents the opportunity to be responsible for their child or children, yet also allows the experience of a significant, routine period of time without children. This may seem irresponsible to some readers; it should be recognized, however, that time away from one's child is a practical advantage of joint custody which may be necessary for a growing number of today's families. In reality, divorce with sole custody may be unworkable for parents who have both assumed significant roles outside of the home. The changes which a sole custody arrangement demand could well be detrimental for both parents and children. For instance, if it was necessary for one parent to stop working because he or she had custody, one result would be a major reduction in the family's source of income. Obviously there are a number of other possible consequences such as frustration, boredom, resentment, etc., which might be detrimental to both the custodial parent and child.

Joint custody is an appealing option for many divorced men and women, in that it allows both parents flexibility in their personal and professional lives. As more women continue to work for economic, personal, and professional reasons and as more men begin to demand participation in childrearing, joint custody may be the most advantageous custody arrangement for increasing numbers of divorcing parents.

POTENTIAL DRAWBACKS FOR CHILDREN AND PARENTS

We have drawn heavily from the available literature about the effects of divorce on children and have attempted to show how joint custody might alleviate some of the problems associated with divorce. In this section we are going to discuss some of the potential negative effects a joint custody arrangement may have for children and parents. Again, the lack of well-researched information makes it necessary to draw from related theories and concepts and at times even to explore conjecture and myth. This enables us to examine both the documented limitations of joint custody and the arguments (which may or may not be valid) that have been used to criticize such custody arrangements. We believe that a parent considering joint custody needs to be aware of both types of information. Realistic knowledge about the potential negative effects of joint custody will help divorcing parents to decide whether it is an appropriate option for their family; knowledge about doubts, rumors, and even myths about the subject can help joint custody families to defend their choice. Equally as important, accurate information will allow them to educate others regarding both actual and imaginary drawbacks of joint custody.

Professionals involved with divorcing families also need to be aware of the potential negative effects of joint custody. In their roles as therapists, advisors, and consultants, professionals may be asked to help divorcing parents to decide if joint custody is in their family's best interest.

Perhaps the strongest objections to joint custody center around the belief that such arrangements may be too disruptive for children. The view is that a child's life may be disrupted both physically and emotionally by a custody arrangement which often results in the child living in two homes. Estelle Rubin and Edith Atkin reason as follows:

> Divided custody generally means disrupting the child's surroundings, his schooling, his social activities, his friendships. Perhaps the most deleterious aspect of divided custody is that it disturbs the continuity of the relationship with either parent. (Atkin and Rubin, 1976:155)

Rubin and Atkin continue:

> We know one eight-year-old girl who, as a solution to the fierce custody battle waged over her, spends one week with one parent, the next week with the other! (The parents live in the same school district, so she attends one school.) Clearly, this arrangement has more to do with the parents' need to keep their own fighting relationship going than with the child's best interests. (Atkin and Rubin, 1976:155)

Vicki Eder, a family court counselor, also stresses the need for stability in a child's life in noting that joint custody

> may be psychologically stressful for very young children (under the age of two) who need consistency and the continuity of a parenting relationship. . . . [And] when used for the convenience of the parent, passing the children back and forth, the stability of the child may suffer. (Eder, 1978: 24–25)

The above arguments stem in part from theories regarding child development. One theoretical framework which has been particularly influential in the area of child custody and placement is psychoanalytic theory. In what is perhaps the most influential book written from a psychoanalytic perspective concerning child custody and placement, authors Gold-

stein, Freud, and Solnit (1973) propose guidelines for adoption, foster placement, and child custody. It is from their
conclusions regarding child custody that may of the objections to joint custody have stemmed. Their book strongly
emphasizes the importance of maintaining continuity in both
a child's *relationships* and a child's *surroundings*. The authors believe that the child's relationship with one parent
—the custodial parent—should not be disturbed. They even
recommend that the noncustodial parent not possess the
legally enforceable right to visit the child or children. This
recommendation has contributed to the belief that sole custody is the only appropriate custody option following divorce. Goldstein, Freud, and Solnit believe that "children
have difficulty in relating positively to, profiting from, and
maintaining the contact with two psychological parents who
are not in positive contact with each other." (Goldstein,
Freud, and Solnit, 1973:38). They also emphasize the need
for a stable and secure environment for the child, stating:

> Physical, emotional, intellectual, social, and moral
> growth does not happen without causing the child in-
> evitable internal difficulties. The instability of all mental
> processes during the period of development needs to be off-
> set by stability and uninterrupted support from external
> sources. Smooth growth is arrested or disrupted when up-
> heavals and changes in the external world are added to the
> internal ones. (Goldstein, Freud, and Solnit, 1973:32)

While we agree that it is important for a custody arrangement to provide stability and continuity in a child's life, we
must take issue with those who have interpreted Goldstein,
Freud, and Solnit to mean that joint custody can never be
an appropriate option. In their most recent book, *Before the
Best Interests of the Child* (1979), Goldstein, Freud, and
Solnit explain that many of their ideas in *Beyond the Best
Interests of the Child* were misunderstood. They contend
that in their discussion of divorce and custody they were referring only to those cases in which parents could not agree

about custody. In *Before the Best Interests of the Child* Goldstein, Freud, and Solnit are concerned about minimizing the states' intervention into family life. They advocate the family's right to develop a custody arrangement based on the family's needs, explaining that state "intervention is justified only when one or both of the separating parents . . . bring to the court their disagreement about custody of the children. A child is thus (a) protected from instrusion if his separating parents can decide to continue to care for him jointly or separately or to entrust his care to a third party;" (Goldstein, Freud and Solnit, 1979 = 31)

Lack of stability and continuity in a child's life are not of course the only potential problems of a joint custody arrangement. Another criticism that has been offered is that it creates a "double bind" situation for a child. Henry Foster, professor of law at New York University and chairman-elect of the American Bar Association's family law section, argues this point: "From the standpoint of the child, the situation is one of divided authority or what's called the double bind —it's a dangerous situation for a child" (Dullea, 1976). Other authors (Atkin and Rubin, 1977; Dullea, 1976; Goldstein et al., 1973; Jenkins, 1977) have also expressed concern about divided parental authority, suggesting that it is unworkable and potentially deleterious for children of divorce. In fact, the contention has been made (Goldstein et al., 1973) that loyalty conflicts are common when children maintain substantial contact with divorced parents.

The child's feeling of having to side with one parent or the other may be particularly problematic in situations where the parents are hostile and argumentative. In such a case, a child may feel caught in the middle, unsure of which way to turn for comfort and support. In relating joint custody to this conflict, Eder writes that "it can become, or continue to be, the source of a power struggle between the parents, with the child caught in the middle (Eder, 1978:21). This argument is based in part on the assumption that the parental conflict experienced before and during the divorce will continue. Roman explains that some authorities feel that

> parents who could not reconcile conflicts while living together are even less likely to be accommodating to one another while living apart and also, that joint custody puts the child in an untenable position, dividing his loyalties, even at times his physical surroundings and minimizing, as a result, his stability. (Roman, 1977:8)

Some of the potential problems of joint custody concern the practical day-to-day effects of such an arrangement. For instance, difficulties may arise when joint custody involves a child living alternately with each parent. A child may have difficulty maintaining peer contacts and school continuity unless the parents live very close to each other. A magazine article on joint custody reported:

> Bruce and Barbara Reinhart of Minneapolis find that joint custody of their daughters, Jennifer, 10, and Amy Jo, 8, is manageable but has drawbacks. "Carting possessions around is tough. . . . Suitcases, nighttime animals, half an outfit here, half there—no steady routine." (*Time*, 1979: 61)

Statements such as this illustrate the daily time and effort which joint custody arrangements may require, and they reflect the frustration children may feel concerning the transition between two homes. While not having the right toy or outfit may seem unimportant to an outsider, parents who have experienced a child's displeasure and confusion when missing a cherished item realize the significance such belongings have for children. When two homes are involved, a parent may not be willing or able to immediately recover the missing object, and the result may well be an upset child and a frazzled parent.

When parents alternate physical custody, the actual moving from one home to the other may in and of itself be un-settling for a child.

> Charles and Anita Josey of Atlanta, Ga., have been shar-ing custody of their seven-year-old son, Allen, for more than three years. Although both parents feel the arrange-ment is on balance beneficial to Allen—and to them—they are beginning to perceive some of its features as drawbacks. "The trouble is, we're constantly bouncing him back and forth. . . . He says he would rather live in one place or the other." (Kellogg, 1977:57)

Many readers may be able to identify with the experience of alternately living in two homes. Two increasingly common examples come to mind in which adults find themselves in a living situation similar to that of many joint custody chil-dren: people living together prior to marriage, often alter-nating between one partner's home and the other's; and married couples who work so far from one another that they maintain two residences. In both examples, reports of this being disconcerting are common enough to make it seem likely that joint custody involving two homes might be un-settling for a child.

The preceding has dealt with the practical problems which may arise when joint custody involves sharing physical custody on a regular and frequent basis. Some of those prob-lems are also likely when the physical custody of a child is shared for longer periods of time. An example would be when one parent has physical custody during the summer and the other has physical custody during the school year. If the parents do not live near each other, the child may find it difficult to maintain consistent contact with friends, since children usually make friends at their school and in their home neighborhood. Earlier we said that the ability to form relationships with peers becomes more important as a child gets older; when he or she reaches school age, and particu-larly during adolescence, parents are no longer the only im-

portant persons in a child's life. Parents who have a joint custody arrangement involving extended physical custody in different geographical locations may find that their child becomes increasingly dissatisfied with the arrangement.

We have seen that children living in joint custody situations may experience problems in several areas. Alternately living in two homes, relating to divided parental authority, and continuing significant contact with parents who have not adequately resolved their marital discords stand out as potential difficulties. Although such problems should be examined and weighed when considering joint custody, they are not of course exclusive to joint custody. For example, a sole custody arrangement which includes significant visitation by the noncustodial parents may result in some if not all of these same problems.

Joint custody arrangements may result in problems for parents as well as for children. A frequent criticism of joint custody is that it is unrealistic to expect divorced parents to be able to make decisions together about their children. Lawyer Harry F. Fain believes that "it's asking a lot to expect two people who could not get along in marriage to suddenly share decision making for a child's educational, religious, and everyday activities" (Dullea, 1976:1). There is an assumption in this argument that parents cannot or will not separate their marital relationship from their parental relationship. Marriage and family counselors contend that it is the parents' ability to separate feelings about the marriage from feelings about their children which in large part determines the success or failure of a joint custody arrangement. The couple's ability to communicate with each other in a productive, comfortable manner is essential, since joint custody not only implies having some contact with a former spouse but also involves negotiation and compromise. The ability to make decisions about a child together requires mutual respect; obviously this is something not all divorcing parents will have. As Charlotte Baum points out, some lawyers believe that parents are incapable of arriving at a mutually acceptable answer when disagreements arise in joint custody arrangements.

> If substantial disagreement occurred—and it probably would, then the only recourse would be for either of us to go to court and ask for sole custody. So why not start out with what we would no doubt end up with—the theory being that parents who couldn't reconcile conflicts while

living together are even less likely to be accommodating to one another while living apart. (Baum, 1976:44)

Two recent New York court cases illustrate the problems that can arise when parents who have a joint custody arrangement cannot cooperate with each other. They also show the willingness of the court to refuse and overturn joint custody awards. In *Dodd* v. *Dodd,* a New York trial court would not award joint custody to a couple who had tried the arrangement during a fourteen month prelitigation period. Explaining its decision, the court said:

> Joint custody has been tried by the Dodd family, and in the court's view it has failed. For fourteen months, the parents have lived apart without either a separation agreement or a court order of custody. During that time they have shared in all decisions, and for most of that time they have divided physical custody equally. In all areas, in matters both major and minor, there has been conflict.... Overt, bitter hostility, criticism of each other, as well as angry words and obscenities have been observed repeatedly by the children. (*Dodd* v. *Dodd*)

In a similar case, *Braiman* v. *Braiman,* the New York Court of Appeals reversed an order of a lower court awarding the couple joint custody of their sons. The court explained its ruling as follows:

> More than four years since their separation, the parents are evidently still unable to manage their common problems with their children, let alone trust each other. Instead, they continue to find fault and accuse. They have failed to work out between themselves even a limited visitation with the children. To expect them to exercise the responsibility entailed in sharing their children's physical custody at this time seems beyond rational hope. It would, moreover, take more than reasonable self restraint to shield the children, as they go from house to house, from the ill feelings, hatred, and disrespect each parent harbors toward the other. (*Braiman* v. *Braiman*)

An argument closely allied with the notion that in a joint custody arrangement parents will be unable to cooperate with each other is that such custody does not allow divorced parents to truly separate from one another. Charlotte Baum writes, "Some psychologists cautioned us that the frequent contact our situation demands would be a way for us to avoid making a complete break and to continue a husband-wife relationship that in their eyes was illegitimate" (Baum, 1976:44). In effect, this statement suggests that joint custody may make it psychologically impossible for formerly married individuals to adequately resolve and terminate their marital relationship. Bruce Johnson, a psychiatric social worker in Chicago, states, "From the kid's point of view, he always has hope that the family will be united. . . . It's the same with the parents—and joint custody doesn't help any of the parties reach that acceptance" (Kellogg, 1977:57).

Although these authorities believe joint custody may interfere with a couple's acceptance of a divorce, others feel that in many instances a divorce is never really final. Gus Napier and Carl Whitaker, two family therapists at the University of Wisconsin-Madison, discuss this:

> We assert that many divorces are merely pieces of legal paper that do little to change the couple's massive entanglement with each other. So many couples are legally divorced but emotionally still married; they simply carry on their marriages internally or through their children. (Napier and Whitaker, 1978:225)

These authors point out the difficulty in divorcing one's spouse when there are children involved, saying that:

> Couples learn that they are "trapped" by their children into a continuing relationship. They may be truly frightened as they realize how profound their ties are to each other, how very difficult it is to get divorced when there are children. (Napier and Whitaker, 1978:229)

Miriam Galper states this position succinctly in the dedication of her book (Galper, 1978) "My marriage has ended and my family continues." Thus whether parents have a joint custody arrangement or not, it is unlikely that they will completely terminate their relationship with one another, particularly those aspects of the relationship which are child-centered.

Joint custody often results in closer contact with one's former spouse than does sole custody. While parents with such custody need not necessarily see each other often, they do need to confer on matters related to the child. Therefore, divorcing parents must ask themselves whether they have the ability and willingness to communicate and cooperate with each other on issues related to childrearing. If the answer is "no," the continued contact necessitated by many joint custody arrangements may well perpetuate or even increase unresolved hostility and resentment (Eder, 1978). We hardly need add that a situation such as this is likely to cause problems for both children and parents.

Like their children, parents may also experience pragmatic, day-to-day problems and inconveniences as a result of joint custody. When children alternate regularly between two homes, the logistics involved in transporting them and their belongings may prove to be time-consuming and inconvenient for parents. Joint custody may also result in additional expenses. For example, if a child regularly lives with each parent, separate bedrooms are needed at both homes. Duplicate sets of certain personal belongings may be necessary, since to some extent a child's sense of well-being and stability is enhanced by familiar surroundings, and some divorcing parents may be unable to afford such a duplication of expenses.

Finally, parents who decide on joint custody may face criticism from family, friends, and the professional community. Both mothers and fathers may find themselves constantly needing to justify their decision as being in the best interests of the child. In discussing reactions of others to her and her husband's plan for joint custody, Charlotte Baum writes: "Lawyers, psychologists, child care authorities, and even friends, warned us that joint custody with dual households couldn't possibly work. Moreover, everyone said, it would be 'hard for the kids' " (Baum, 1976:44) .

Criticism may be especially pronounced from those family members, friends, and professionals who continue to believe that the preferred parent is the mother. Although, as we have discussed, fathers are beginning to be seen as fully capable of caring for their children, maternal preference in childrearing is still quite pronounced. Marshall Hamilton writes:

> The most common tendency in statements about the father's influence is to underestimate it. The studies of absent or inadequate fathers show that even minimal behavior of the father is not completely lacking in influence, but instead is generally a negative one which helps to influence some of the children's characteristics away from the norm in an undesirable direction. Yet statements suggesting that the father has very little or no influence are numerous, while overestimates are rare. (Hamilton, 1977: 145)

The ignorance surrounding fathers and their contributions to childrearing has a negative effect on perceptions of joint custody; it has contributed to the perpetuation of myths regarding maternal preference in child custody cases. Meyer Elkin lists some of the fallacious assumptions often followed in regard to divorce and custody, three of which are of particular relevance to the notion of maternal preference:

1. There is a maternal instinct which automatically makes the woman more competent to rear children.
2. Men cannot be as nurturing and caring to children as women.
3. Children need a mother more than a father. (Elkin, 1978: 16–17)

Assumptions such as these discredit the feasibility and advisability of joint custody, since they imply that fathers are not equal to mothers in either their ability to parent or their importance in parenting. If these assumptions are not challenged, they will undoubtedly result in a bias against joint custody of children.

In this chapter we have explored the potential benefits and drawbacks of joint custody arrangements. Parents considering joint custody will want to use this information to decide whether it is a workable option in their particular situation, asking themselves also, of course, whether it is in the best interests of their children.

6

How to Start

In the previous chapters we have discussed what joint custody is, how it evolved, and its potential strengths and weaknesses. In this chapter we will present specific information about how to obtain joint custody. We have chosen to present this material in the second person, anticipating that its greatest interest may be for those directly contemplating such a custody arrangement. We have included interviews with an attorney and a clinical psychologist to illustrate various points discussed in the chapter.

Any couple in the midst of separation and divorce is likely to experience communication problems. Anger, depression, and confusion are normal reactions to the divorce process. These feelings are likely to interfere with the ability to communicate in a productive and comfortable manner with your spouse. Consequently, discussing the issue of custody will be difficult in many cases; there is probably no other issue more likely to create or rekindle painful feelings. Although couples may try to avoid it, the question of who will have custody of the children can easily evolve into a power struggle. Often the real subject—custody—becomes lost among a myriad of unrelated and unresolved issues which parents may attempt to resolve through arguing or bargaining about care of the children. When this occurs, both parents and children suffer. Children may find themselves in the midst of parental hostility, fear, and confusion. Thus the temptation to use the issue of child custody to resolve other issues or to harm one's spouse must be avoided.

A successful joint custody arrangement necessitates a relationship between parents based on mutual respect. The ability to communicate with each other is essential. It is highly unlikely that joint custody will work if one or both parents find themselves unable or unwilling to talk to the other. Therefore the first step in the process of obtaining joint custody involves examining your feelings about your spouse. We are not suggesting that you should have only positive feelings toward him or her; that is unlikely. But you must both feel a desire and ability to communicate honestly and openly about your children. Even if you do feel willing to discuss childrearing matters, it is likely to be very stressful. Old, unpleasant feelings related to your marriage may be reexperienced, and it may be difficult just to be in close physical proximity to your former spouse. So, initially at least, these times together may be uncomfortable and emotionally draining.

The next step is to discuss with each other the relative merits and problems of different custody arrangements. We assume that prior to doing this you will have spent some time thinking about such matters yourself. You might begin by considering the options in broad terms, asking for example: What are the benefits for myself and my children if I have sole custody? If my former spouse has sole custody? If the two of us have joint custody? It is beneficial to openly discuss all of the possible alternatives together. If you are only willing to discuss one option, arguments may ensue. For instance, if one parent begins the discussion by saying that he or she wants custody, the other parent is immediately put on the defensive. Even if the other believes that this is the best arrangement, he or she may initially feel the need to disagree. The parent who introduces the discussion by suggesting that you consider all the different custody alternatives, acknowledges that there are choices available and indicates that both are "good parents." This acknowledgment implies that there is mutual respect. Once this has been established, discussion can center around the potential positive and negative effects of various custody arrangements.

The process of considering the possible solutions or alternatives to a given situation is sometimes called brainstorming, or creative problem solving. Brainstorming is a helpful technique, encouraging creativity and cooperation. It allows all possible alternatives to be expressed without passing judgment as to which are good and which are bad. It is only after all alternatives have been listed that each should be discussed and evaluated. Brainstorming can sometimes result in a solution that neither parent had previously considered. The following guideline might be used to facilitate brainstorming about child custody alternatives.

1. Parents agree to meet and discuss custody of their children.
2. Each parent privately makes a list of all the possible child custody arrangements.
3. Using a blackboard or large piece of paper, one parent writes down one of the possible arrangements he or she has thought of; the other then does the same. The parents continue alternating until they have exhausted their respective lists. A short explanation of each other's alternatives can then be offered. However, the discussion should focus only on explaining the concept —arguing for or against it should be avoided at this time.
4. When all of the listed alternatives have been written down, any other idea belatedly thought of can be added.
5. When all ideas have been noted on the common list, each parent should copy them down for his or her own use.
6. Parents should take this new list home, think about the

alternatives, evaluate them, and be prepared to discuss all of the options at the next meeting.

7. Parents should arrange to meet together again. At this session they should evaluate the alternatives together, eliminating those that both feel are unacceptable; this begins the process of narrowing down potential custody choices.

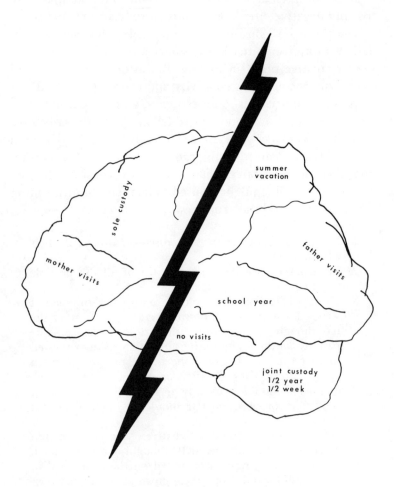

This brainstorming technique ought to provide a framework which minimizes conflict but generates several potential solutions. For example, it could result in the following list of possible alternatives. This list is of course in no way meant to be inclusive.

1. Sole custody with mother, father will visit.
2. Sole custody with mother, father will not visit.
3. Sole custody with father, mother will visit.
4. Sole custody with father, mother will not visit.
5. Joint custody, child lives with mother.
6. Joint custody, child lives with father.
7. Joint custody, child lives half of the week with mother and half of the week with father.
8. Joint custody, child lives half of the year with mother and half of the year with father.
9. Joint custody, child lives with mother during school year and with father in summer.

It is unlikely that you and your spouse will be able to reach a decision regarding custody during your first or even second meeting. You may find it useful to agree ahead of time to discuss only child custody during these times, since that may minimize contaminating the conversation with other unresolved and potentially hostile feelings. You may find in the course of these discussions that you or your spouse need more information about joint custody. If this is the case, we suggest sharing this book or other pertinent literature (we have provided a bibliography at the back), talking to people who have joint custody, or discussing the subject with knowledgeable professionals.

If you do decide to pursue joint custody, there are several courses of action to follow. First, you may consider trying a joint custody arrangement while you are separated and not yet divorced. Let us assume, as in many separations, that one parent has remained with the children in the home while the other has moved to another residence. It may be possible to arrange the situation so that you can practice your joint custody arrangement before the divorce hearing. For instance, if one of the goals of your joint custody arrangement is to equally share the physical presence of your child, you could begin to do so during the separation period. However, because this time is often very stressful for children, there are several factors you should consider. One issue is the physical proximity of the child's two homes. Ideally, the parents should live close enough to each other to insure that the child's continuity with his or her friends, school, and neighborhood is not disturbed. While alternately living with each parent may not be easy for the child, the continued contact with both may well outweigh the disadvantages of moving between two homes. To lessen stress on the child, a preferred alternative during the separation period might be for the parents to alternate homes. This would allow for a greater sense of continuity during an already difficult period in a child's life. We are not suggesting that this arrangement necessarily continue over a long period of time; the parents' relationship with other adults may inevitably lead to the infeasibility of this type of arrangement. If your joint custody arrangement includes sharing physical custody of the child, your child will most likely have to learn to make the transition between your home and your former spouse's home.

There are two very real advantages to using the separation period to test out a joint custody arrangement. First, you will then be in a better position to evaluate the positive and negative effects of this type of arrangement. You and your family may find joint custody to be a very satisfactory arrangement, or you may decide that it is totally unworkable. Another possibility is that you may find such custody has the potential to be successful if certain modifications in the arrangement are made. Regardless of any preliminary assumptions, you and your spouse will have had first-hand experience from which to evaluate your joint custody arrangement. A second benefit of trying it during your separation period is that this may increase the possibility that joint custody will be viewed favorably by the court. The ability to say honestly to a judge that your family has been functioning under this type of custody arrangement during your separation and that you understand the complexities of the arrangement but feel that it is in the best interest of all involved, may increase the likelihood of joint custody being awarded to you and your former spouse. While we are not suggesting that it is mandatory to have practiced joint custody prior to the divorce hearings, we do maintain that it is often beneficial in positively influencing the court. More importantly, practicing this arrangement during your separation period will help you and your family formulate an accurate opinion about joint custody.

Another step in the process of obtaining joint custody involves choosing an attorney. Your and your spouse's attorney is the person who will guide you through the divorce and custody process. Therefore, this choice is an important decision, deserving careful consideration. There are several ways in which you can increase the likelihood of choosing an attroney who will be knowledgeable and supportive in regard to joint custody.

First, it is to your advantage to choose someone who has divorce and custody experience. This may seem self-evident, but you may not realize that certain attorneys specialize in legal matters unrelated to divorce and custody and may rarely handle divorce cases. Because joint custody is relatively new and controversial, it is wise to choose a lawyer who has a special interest and expertise in the area of divorce and child custody. Ideally of course, you would like your attorney to have had experience with joint custody. If this is not possible, then choose an attorney who is at least informed about it and believes it is in the best interests of some divorcing families. Don't be afraid to ask an attorney how he or she feels about this custody alternative, since it would be ridiculous to hire one who is vehemently against the idea. In summary, it will be to your advantage to choose an attorney who is knowledgeable about joint custody, supportive of families who decide on this alternative, and willing and interested in helping you obtain such a custody arrangement.

There are numerous ways to locate such a person. Perhaps the easiest is to simply ask your divorced friends, colleagues, or neighbors about their attorneys. It is particularly helpful to speak with someone who has gained joint custody, asking them who their attorney was and whether they were satisfied with the services they received. We found that most people who have joint custody are eager to talk about their experiences and are interested in helping other families who are considering such custody. Another way to find an appropriate attorney is by contacting the local bar association; often they have a referral service. While in the process of writing this book, we called the Wisconsin bar association in Madison, Wisconsin, and were given the names of four attorneys who handled joint custody cases. Your own local bar association may not be able to provide you with names of attorneys who have handled joint custody cases, but you can at least expect to be referred to attorneys who specialize in divorce and custody.

In addition to attorneys, there are other professionals who may be of help to you in securing joint custody of your child or children. For instance, if you and your spouse have been seeing a counselor or therapist, it might be wise to continue doing so while you are in the process of obtaining joint custody. Planning and implementing this custody decision will require additional contact with your former spouse; consequently, an objective party may be beneficial. A counselor or therapist could help mediate disputes, offer support and suggestions, assist you in gaining insight into the situation, and in general guide the divorce and joint custody process along. If you have already been seeing a counselor or therapist, it may be necessary to renegotiate your agreement about the objectives of your sessions—that is, to consider whether you now want to focus sessions on issues related to joint custody.

Some couples do not seek out a counselor until they have decided they will divorce. Often they do so to help make the separation easier, to assist them with issues related to divorce and custody, or to grow and learn from the divorce experience. People who enlist a counselor or therapist during this time usually hope to gain support, advice, and insight about this immense change in their lives.

One should consider some of the same factors when choosing a therapist as were mentioned in the reference to selecting an attorney. For instance, consider whether the therapist or counselor is knowledgeable and experienced in helping people through the divorce process, in issues related to custody, and in the area of child growth and development. It is also important to consider whether or not both spouses feel they are able to relate personally to the counselor and vice versa. The therapist may want to include the child or children in the sessions, and this is often a very appropriate and profitable plan of action. Well-known family therapists Gus Napier and Carl Whitaker believe that children should always be involved in family therapy sessions. They explain:

> When the issue is divorce, membership at the meetings can be complicated. As always, the children are involved; they need to understand why the divorce is occurring, to be perfectly clear that it is not their fault, and to be reassured that both parents will remain in their lives. (Napier and Whitaker, 1978:26)

A good counselor or therapist can help families cope with and even profit from the experience of divorce. We are not suggesting that all divorcing couples need to see a counselor or therapist. For some, however, such assistance may be personally valuable; in addition, it could have a pragmatic use, since it will be to your benefit to have the support of a respected counselor or therapist when your case for joint custody is heard in court.

While professionals such as lawyers and mental health workers may be of immense help while you are considering joint custody, so also may families who have already obtained such a custody arrangement. Talking to people who have joint custody is one obvious means of gaining information and insight. Although it may not be easy to find such families, relying on common sense and utilizing familiar resources will undoubtedly help. Simply letting other people know that you are looking for families who have joint custody is a first step. Your friends, family, or co-workers may themselves have joint custody or may be able to provide you with names of people who have. Contacting established groups in the community might also be productive; for instance, you might call the president of the local Parents Without Partners chapter and ask if any of their members have joint custody and if so, whether they would either be willing to release the names or have those members contact you. Local religious organizations sponsoring discussion groups about single parenting may also be able to assist you in locating families who have joint custody.

These are just a few suggestions as to how to find families with joint custody arrangements. Talking with families who already have such custody may be a very valuable experience, but we caution you not to rely solely on this information when making a decision about it. The life experiences, needs, desires, and present situation of another family may be very different from your own; thus some of the information you receive may not be applicable to your family. However, practical details such as who their attorney was, what the agreement included, and what they would have done differently may be useful information which could apply to a wide spectrum of people. You will undoubtedly want to ask what positive and negative effects a family has experienced as a result of joint custody. But again, remember that it is their arrangement; the problems and benefits they cite may not apply to you and your family.

An Interview with John Albert, an Attorney Who Has Joint Custody

John Albert is a practicing attorney in Madison, Wisconsin. After seven years of marriage, John and his wife were divorced. They developed a joint custody agreement, and for the past three years have had joint custody of their two children, a four-year-old boy and a seven-year-old girl.

MEL: John, I'm curious about why you decided to pursue a joint custody arrangement.

JOHN: I guess the reason it evolved as joint custody was a real unwillingness on my part to be physically separated from the kids for any length of time. I didn't want to be the type of divorced father who showed up at ten o'clock on Saturday or Sunday and said, "Today we're going to the zoo or a Walt Disney movie." I wanted the kids to know me as a father figure, to see me in less than a happy mood in the morning sometimes, to see me get up and go to work and basic things like that.

MEL: What happened next?

JOHN: My former wife and I discussed the possibility of her having sole custody or of my having sole custody. We went through the normal recriminations: "You're doing this to me, so I'm keeping the children...." This was never said out in the open, but it was there.

When we separated, my wife decided to move out and get an apartment downtown. I kept the kids at our house for over three months. When she came to visit the kids, I usually needed and wanted to get away for awhile, so I would leave. What happened, though unintentioned, was that the kids got used to spending time with one parent or the other. In retrospect it was like an adjustment period that gave us a chance to get used to this type of arrangement.

MEL: So you are in some ways suggesting that people in the process of divorce who are considering joint custody could begin the process during their separation?

JOHN: Exactly. I didn't realize it then, but I see it now. That transition period was really beneficial. I think a great deal of trauma for kids in divorce comes from the old,

"Sheriff knocks at the door and all of a sudden Daddy's gone." The kids never forget it.

MEL: Since you were awarded joint custody before there was a law in Wisconsin, how did you know about it? Did you know about this option because you are a lawyer?

JOHN: As I remember, it was a solution that we arrived at to meet our own needs. Even if we were required by law to have sole custody, we were going to live by a joint custody arrangement. It was a conscious decision on our part to do with our lives and our kids' lives what we felt was in all of our best interests. Fortunately, a woman in the family court commissioners office knew about joint custody, was excited about it, and helped us work out an agreement which the courts would accept.

MEL: Just a bit about the specifics of your joint custody agreement. You have the kids one half of the time and she has them the other half?

JOHN: Right. We've been doing this for over two years now. We live within a few blocks of each other, and we each have the kids for one half of the week.

MEL: Since joint custody was a new idea when you were awarded it, how did you get the courts to accept the idea?

JOHN: Well, the fact that as an attorney I know the family court system certainly helped. I suspected that certain judges would be more willing to accept and support this arrangement, so I tried to see that the case was heard by that kind of judge.

MEL: There might be a lesson here for anyone considering joint custody. You need to be a good consumer. That is, by getting to know something about the people in the court system, you'll have a better chance for success.

JOHN: Unfortunately, personalities, beliefs, etc., do play a part. I knew that there were certain judges who would look askance at anything this new, and certain judges who would likely be favorable. The situation will probably be similar in other parts of the country. The couple's attorney or attorneys can help by their knowledge of the legal system in their area.

MEL: Since joint custody, like any custody decision, must be okayed by the courts, how would you prepare a couple who wanted joint custody for court? What kind of information would they need to know?

JOHN: First, they would need to explore realistic financial and physical arrangements. If these were really out of line, they might consider changing them. It might, for instance, be necessary for one parent to move, or for one to agree to pay some child support, etc.

MEL: What about the distance one parent lives from the other —how important do you feel this is?

JOHN: I think that it's very important if the parents will be sharing the kids' physical presence equally or almost equally. If you live miles from each other, continuity for the kids in terms of friends and school is difficult. If you live close and one kid forgets a favorite toy, blanket, etc., you can get it quickly. If you had to drive ten miles to get it, chances are you would try to convince the kid to get through the night without it. Blankets and favorite things can be very important to three-year-old kids. Also, considering things like these and showing that you have made realistic arrangements will probably help in court.

MEL: What about the actual joint custody agreement? What did you put in yours? What would you advise other people to put in their agreements?

JOHN: A joint custody agreement is really an opportunity for a couple to creatively plan a custody arrangement based on their specific needs. Because my former wife and I felt that geographic distance was important, we put in a provision that if either party moved outside of Madison, the agreement would have to be reviewed by the courts. We also included a provision for voluntarily submitting major disagreements to the family court counseling service for resolution. Though their decision would not necessarily be binding, it is an attempt to anticipate problems that might arise and ways to solve potential problems. So far we haven't had to use that part of our agreement.

MEL: But you believe that it is useful to include a way to handle major disagreements?

JOHN: Right, a trusted counselor, religious figure, etc.

MEL: If the disagreement continues, is it possible to go back to the court for final resolution?

JOHN: It is, but I think people would want to avoid this if at all possible. First, it will likely take some time and possibly a long time to actually get back into court. Second, it will involve some financial burden if, as is likely, lawyers are involved.

MEL: Getting back to preparing people for a successful court appearance. Is it important to involve outside experts like counselors, therapists, etc.?

JOHN: It can be very helpful. If, for instance, the couple was seeing a counselor to help work out the details of the divorce, including counseling around the issue of joint custody would be helpful. Remember, judges follow the "best interests of the child" guideline, and it will always be helpful if someone with expertise in child development is willing to say that they have talked with you about the issues and feel joint custody is a good plan.

AN INTERVIEW WITH DR. JAMES LEWIS, A FAMILY THERAPIST

Dr. James Lewis is a clinical psychologist in private practice. Dr. Lewis has been a family therapist for more than twenty-five years. Recently he has worked with several families who have decided on and implemented joint custody following divorce.

MEL: In your family counseling practice you've seen several joint custody families?

JIM: Right, both when there was an informal joint custody agreement before the divorce, and after the couples were awarded joint custody. The first case I was involved with was about five years ago. A couple wanted to share custody, but the court initially said no. The couple was told by the court to sit down together and decide which parent would have custody. It was a terrible experience for them, and therapeutically it was destructive.

MEL: Because they wanted to share custody, but the court insisted they decide which of them would have sole custody?

JIM: That was part of it. By insisting that they work through the question themselves, the couple was put in an impossible situation.

MEL: Are you saying that by themselves people can't decide upon a custody arrangement?

JIM: For this couple that was the case. It isn't true for all couples. These people were at an impasse because they both wanted custody. The psychological symbolism of custody was very important.

MEL: What was custody a symbol of for this couple?

JIM: Like so many couples, they felt that whoever had custody had control and power. This feeling created a rivalry between the parents. Whoever got custody would be the winner and the other the loser. Fortunately, we were able to work out a shared custody arrangement. The parents were cooperative, even though there was still a lot of anger about their divorce. However, they were able to overcome that and work out a relationship that was good for their little girl. We finally got the court to go along with this, and the couple was awarded legal joint custody.

MEL: How is the daughter doing in this joint custody arrangement?

JIM: Beautifully. I still see the family about twice a year. The girl has adjusted well; there have been no major problems.

MEL: Let's take a hypothetical case. A couple comes to see you because they are getting a divorce and they want to have some type of joint custody arrangement. What clues would you look for that might make you think this couple will or won't have a successful joint custody arrangement?

JIM: Underlying everything else is the question: Are they able to communicate? Can they develop a system of communication which will allow them to talk about the needs of their child? This is the base upon which successful joint custody can be built. Then I'd want each parent to get in touch with their motivation for wanting joint custody. I'd want to make sure they're really thinking about the child's best interest. It's important to keep the focus on the kids. Parents need to be certain that they are not going to use their children like pawns to fight back and forth.

MEL: How do children benefit from joint custody?

JIM: Obviously, the major benefit is that they still have two parents. I believe that kids grow in a healthier way and function better if they have exposure to both parents. I think it's very important that following divorce parents keep in close contact with their children; joint custody provides a vehicle to do this.

MEL: You say that joint custody helps keep parents in close contact with their children. Some parents work this out informally; do you think having legal joint custody is important?

JIM: Definitely. For some couples it can be very important to have the judge say, "You have joint custody." Psychologically it is important for some divorcing parents to feel equal concerning their children. Using the words "joint custody" reaffirms that neither parent is losing custody of their child.

MEL: Have there been any other issues concerning joint custody you have encountered?

JIM: An interesting issue that comes up time and time again in divorce is the grandparents' relationship with the child. Often grandparents fear that after divorce they won't be able to see their grandchild. Kids need grandparents, they can play an important role in child development. Joint custody can be important to the grandparents by alleviating this fear of losing their grandchild. While this isn't a reason to pursue joint custody, it is an additional benefit of this custody arrangement.

MEL: How would you summarize your experience with joint custody families?

JIM: In some ways joint custody takes more work than sole custody. To be successful, divorcing parents must be able to be in regular contact with their exspouse, talk about their children's needs, and make sure they don't put the child in the middle of their unresolved problems. I think for those parents willing and able to make joint custody work, the benefits justify the effort. Ideally, you'll have a well adjusted child and happier parents.

7

The Joint Custody Agreement

A part of the legal divorce agreement must include a discussion or stipulation regarding child custody. Since courts view one of their major functions as protecting children who are involved in divorce, the custody section of the divorce agreement is very important. If divorcing parents want joint custody, an agreement must be developed which specifies what joint custody means and how it will work in their specific case. In essence, such an agreement is a written, legally binding description of the way the couple will function with joint custody following their divorce. As such, there is no single proper or correct joint custody agreement; rather, each one should be designed to reflect the special needs and desires of a particular family. We have argued throughout this book that one reason that joint custody is an exciting and innovative custody arrangement is that it allows each divorcing family sufficient flexibility to plan for its specific needs. Parents can design an agreement which best maximizes the potential for positive growth and development of all family members.

Although every joint custody agreement is unique to a

specific family, there are common issues and questions which most divorcing parents will want to address. In addition, there are specific items that virtually every court will insist be included. In this chapter we will discuss how the joint custody agreement can be developed. We are not attempting to give legal advice; obviously this should be provided by the couple's attorney (s) . We wish only to suggest areas and issues that divorcing parents should consider including in their joint custody agreement.

We have gathered information for this chapter by utilizing several different sources. These include reviewing numerous joint custody agreements, talking to joint custody families and attorneys about the development of their agreements, and borrowing ideas from Stephen M. Gaddis's excellent article (Gaddis, 1978) . After discussing the development of the joint custody agreement, we will reprint two agreements that have been used in actual divorce cases.

DEFINITION OF JOINT CUSTODY

Most agreements will begin by explaining why the parents are requesting joint custody. The basic intent of the arrangement can also be addressed in this section. Many joint custody agreements begin by recognizing that both parents are fit and proper persons. Consider the positive wording of an Oregon agreement (printed in its entirety at the end of this chapter) , which states, "We believe each of us to be fit parents and recognize the unique contribution each of us has to offer our children." Another example is a Wisconsin agreement, beginning, "Inasmuch as both parties recognizes that each of them is a fit and proper person to have the care, custody, and control of the minor child. . . ."

The agreement may then proceed by defining joint custody. Divorcing parents may decide on a specific or more general definition of the arrangement. The Oregon agreement reads:

We wish to continue to share responsibility for the care of the children and each fully participate in all major decisions affecting their health, education and welfare, while disrupting their life patterns as little as possible.

Stephen M. Gaddis suggests the following:

It is the intention of the parents in agreeing to joint legal custody, that each of them shall continue having a full and active role in providing a sound moral, social, economic, and educational environment for the children. ... The parents shall consult with one another in substantial questions relating to religious upbringing, educational programs, significant changes in social environment, and non-emergency health care of the children. In accepting the broad grant of privileges conferred by this joint custodial arrangement upon each parent, they specifically recognize that these powers shall not be exercised for the purpose of frustrating, denying, or controlling in any manner the social development of the other parent. The parents shall exert their best efforts to work cooperatively in future plans consistent with the best interests for the children and in amiably resolving such disputes as may arise. (Gaddis, 1978:20)

PHYSICAL CUSTODY OF THE CHILD

In this part of the agreement, the parents will address the question of when, where, and with whom the child will reside. Since a joint custody agreement can encompass any of a number of physical custody arrangements, this issue of custody will need to be dealt with fully in this section.

If the child is to spend equal or at least a significant amount of time with each parent, there are several ways such an arrangement can be delineated. Parents may decide to be very specific about physical custody in their agreement, stating, for example, "The child shall spend the first half of the month with his mother and the second half of the month with his father." Another agreement may be more general and read, "it is contemplated that physical custody of the child shall be fairly equal, considerations being given to the need of the minor child. Specific days and times with a given parent shall be worked out and agreed on by each parent with a view toward providing continuity and predictability in their lives, and with a view toward the best interest of the child."

In some cases parents may agree that one will have sole physical custody of the children, while the other will have visitation rights. This kind of arrangement should also be discussed in this section of the custody agreement.

The decision whether to be very specific or more general in this section should depend upon several factors. First, and most important, is what will be most helpful to the family. While a general agreement allows for more flexibility, it also has the potential for more disagreement. There are certainly families for which such a trade-off would be beneficial. For instance, if one parent's work results in frequent out-of-town travel with little forewarning, the entire family may benefit from the flexibility of a broad, loosely defined understanding of the physical custody arrangement. However, it is crucial that if the physical custody is to be flexible, both parents must be comfortable with this arrangement. If either parent is dissatisfied with it, there is a danger that physical custody may become a battleground with the child trapped in the middle. Even if both parents are satisfied with a flexible arrangement, it is important to the child's sense of well-being that stability and consistency be present. This does not mean that the written joint custody agreement must be highly specific, but that the parents should attempt to develop a physical custody arrangement which can most often be followed. Frequent changes in the usual living arrangement schedule would certainly not be in the child's best interests.

Families who can anticipate a routine pattern of lifestyle may benefit from a more specific—though not necessarily rigid—physical custody provision in their agreement. One major consideration in deciding how specific or flexible to make your agreement is the requirements of the court. Your attorney can advise you about the court's willingness or unwillingness to consider various physical custody arrangements.

A third type of physical custody provision is one which describes a custody arrangement where the child spends a significant amount of time with one parent and then a significant amount of time with the other parent. "The minor child will reside with his mother during the school year and his father during summer vacation," is one such possible manifestation of the physical custody arrangement. This possibility, often referred to as alternating physical custody, can be especially useful when the parents live so far from one another that transporting the child to and from the same school is unrealistic.

FINANCIAL RESPONSIBILITY

Custody arrangements typically include a provision related to the financial responsibilities of the parents for the child. Questions such as who is responsible for the child's health insurance; education; expenses such as babysitting, day care, etc.; and who is entitled to the income tax exemption for the minor child are answered in this section. In addition, the issue of child support is often discussed. It is possible that one parent may pay more for child support than the other in a joint custody arrangement for several reasons. One is that if the joint custody arrangement does not include shared physical custody, the childrearing expenses of one parent are likely to be greater than those of the other. Child support can be used to equalize this inequity. A second reason is that even where the child's physical custody is shared equally, one parent's income may be significantly greater than the other's. In such a situation, all of the arguments and counterarguments about child support may apply—a discussion of which is beyond the scope of this book. However, we do believe it would be disadvantageous for a child who lives with each parent to alternate between an opulent lifestyle and one of financial sparsity. Child support may in such cases be in the child's as well as the parents' best interests.

Mediation and Arbitration

Since joint custody usually means joint decision making, including a section on resolving major disagreements which may arise will be useful. Although the courts are not likely to insist upon a mediator or arbitrator, joint custody couples will be wise to decide upon a mechanism for handling differences of opinion that could become serious problems. A skilled, trusted, professional counselor, agency, or clergyperson are potential arbitrators or mediators. Of course, both parents must agree on the person or agency and feel confident that the chosen mediator or arbitrator is unbiased.

Mediation and arbitration are different processes. In mediation, a third party attempts to help both parties agree upon a mutual decision; the mediator is thus acting as a facilitator between the two parents. If mediation fails to produce a satisfactory agreement, arbitration may be useful. In arbitration, a third party decides which course of action to follow after hearing the wishes of both parents. When parents agree to arbitration, they have in essence agreed to allow a third party to decide for them, since they are unable to reach a decision themselves. Neither mediation nor arbitration legally prevents one parent from returning to court, although the intent is clearly to prevent this course of action.

Couples who include this provision in their agreement should agree to submit major disagreements to a mediator or arbitrator prior to any attempt of either party to have the problem resolved by the courts. Stephen Gaddis reminds us that, "an important part of the joint custodial process is to encourage private decision making rather than litigation" (Gaddis, 1978:26). He suggests adding the following language to the joint custody agreement:

> In the event that the parents alone cannot resolve a conflict, they agree to seek appropriate, competent assistance.

The matter shall be referred for mediation (if that is not successful, for arbitration) to Family Court, a counselor, or to a lawyer or professional person skilled in the resolution of the problems of children and their families. This procedure shall be followed to its conclusion prior to either party seeking relief from the Court. (And: While the dispute is being resolved, the residential parent shall continue making such day to day decisions as are necessary, but shall take no substantial action in the area of the disagreement which would prejudice or take unfair advantage of the other parent by use of the residential status to his/her own benefit.) (Gaddis, 1978:26)

OTHER SECTIONS

The specific idiosyncratic needs and desires of the divorcing family can be accommodated by including additional sections in the joint custody agreement. One strategy the couple might use in deciding whether additional sections are necessary is to ask themselves whether there are any potential issues or concerns that might interfere with their desire or ability to continue with joint custody that have been left unstated. You may remember that John Albert explained in the interview that his agreement contained a stipulation that if either parent moved outside the city limits, the agreement would be open to renegotiation. Because Mr. Albert's joint custody arrangement called for equal physical custody, he and his wife agreed that the close physical proximity of the parents was important; consequently, they decided to renegotiate their agreement if either were to move outside of the city where they both live.

Remarriage, major illness, and significant changes in living arrangements are examples of concern or events that parents may want to consider including in their custody agreement.

SUMMARY

A joint custody agreement is the legal document which details a divorcing family's custody arrangement. The specific content of the agreement will depend upon the needs and desires of the divorcing family and the requirements of the court. A well thought-out agreement has the potential to maximize the chances that joint custody will be successful by minimizing the areas for later disagreement. Although the couple's attorney (s) will be responsible for the specific wording of the agreement, the parents themselves should consider what areas they feel are important and want included. A balance of creativity and practicality should insure that the agreement will be useful for the divorcing family and acceptable to the court.

SAMPLE AGREEMENTS

This chapter concludes with two actual examples of joint custody agreements. These are actual agreements that have been used in joint custody cases. We remind the reader that they should be considered only as samples, not as rigid models. Since these agreements were integrated into overall divorce agreements, we have reprinted only the parts that deal specifically with joint custody; this has necessitated minor reorganization. We have also made small changes to insure anonymity.

A JOINT CUSTODY AGREEMENT*

We, Bob and Barbara Jackson, are husband and wife. We have two children of our marriage: Steve Jackson, age 10, here referred to as Steve, and Carol Jackson, age 9, here referred to as Carol.

Irreconcilable differences have arisen between us causing the irremediable breakdown of our marriage. We intend to seek a dissolution. Bob has, by mutual agreement, moved from the family home in which Barbara and the children continue to reside.

We believe each of us to be fit parents and recognize the unique contribution each of us has to offer our children.

---

*Reprinted with permission of Jay Folberg, attorney and Professor of Law, Lewis and Clark College, Northwestern School of Law.

We wish to continue to share responsibility for the care of the children and each fully participate in all major decisions affecting their health, education and welfare, while disrupting their life patterns as little as possible. We intend to seek joint custody of our children and propose only the most minimal necessary formality in scheduling time with them, subject to consideration of schedules and the necessity of reasonable notice, in order to retain a flexible opportunity for each of us to be with the children and help raise them. Our primary concern has been and shall be the best interests of our children within the reality of our marital dissolution.

We have reached this mutual agreement voluntarily by the process of mediation through a neutral attorney, Jay Folberg. We understand that the mediator was not representing either or both of us.

In consideration of the promises made by each of us to the other, it is agreed between us as follows:

1. Bob and Barbara shall share joint custody of Steve and Carol.

2. Steve and Carol shall reside with Barbara as further set forth below.

3. Should any change of circumstance occur materially affecting the care of the children or Bob's access to them, the residence of Steve and Carol shall be reconsidered in light of then existing circumstances. Should either Bob or Barbara move from the Portland area or change jobs, every effort shall be made to facilitate the continued exercise of joint custody so that the children shall continue to enjoy the benefit of both parents. In considering future living arrangements for the children, Bob and Barbara shall have regard for the children's preference and the environment and care which each can provide.

4. It is anticipated that Bob, as well as Barbara, shall spend regular and considerable time with the children. Bob shall be with the children and responsible for their care at least six days and six nights per month, which shall include one weekend (Friday night, Saturday, Saturday night and Sunday), the time and arrangements for which shall be agreed upon no later than the 25th day of the preceding month. Bob shall be responsible for the children at least one entire week during each of the months of March, June,

July and August, the time and arrangements for which
shall be agreed upon by the 25th day of the preceding
month. Bob shall also spend time with the children, when
possible, on their birthdays and during major holidays.

5. It is expressly understood that the above numerated
times that Bob shall be with the children and responsible
for their immediate care are minimums. Barbara's changing work assignments and Bob's career objectives require
flexibility in child care responsibilities and parental involvement. The terms of this agreement are to be liberally
interpreted to allow the child the maximum benefit to be
derived from the love, concern and care of both Bob and
Barbara.

6. Bob shall pay to Barbara $250 per month toward the
support of each child, payable on the 1st of each month
commencing July 1, 1978. The parties agree that payments
will be made by checking account deposits pursuant to
ORS 23.807–809. Bob's obligation to pay to Barbara $250
per month support for each child shall continue until that
child reaches eighteen years old or comes to reside regularly
with Bob. Fifty dollars of each $250 per month child sup-
port payment shall be set aside in a fund to cover the expenses of tutoring, lessons, camp, medical expenses not
covered by insurance and other special activities for the
children, all as mutually agreed by the parents. Should
either or both children regularly reside with Bob, it shall
be his responsibility to modify the above provided support
provisions, and any decree based upon it.

7. Should both children reside regularly with Bob, Barbara shall pay to Bob such amount toward the support of
each child as her training and employment will allow, but
such amount shall not be less than $100 per month per
child.

8. Bob shall regularly pay to the children, or for their
benefit, necessary amounts for each of their support, maintenance, books and tuition while each is under 21 years
of age and a student regularly attending as a full-time
student, school, community college, college or university,
or regularly attending a course of vocational or technical
training designed to prepare them for gainful employment. Barbara shall also contribute to the support and
expenses of each child between the ages of 18 and 21 while
the child attends school.

9. Bob shall maintain comprehensive medical care insurance for the children.

10. Bob shall keep current insurance on his life in an amount of not less than $100,000 with the children as beneficiaries until they reach the age of twenty-one, for the purpose of receiving their support and expenses to that age.

11. Bob shall, for each child whom he pays support as agreed above, be entitled to the dependency exemption for that child on his federal and state income tax returns.

12. Bob shall pay to Barbara for her support and maintenance $500 per month commencing July 1, 1978 and continuing for a period of 24 months. This obligation shall terminate if Barbara dies or remarries before the expiration of 24 months.

13. The parties will attempt to work together to avoid any further disputes. Shall any dispute arise which we cannot resolve, we wish to avoid the expense and acrimony of formal court proceedings. Therefore, any controversy arising out of or relating to this agreement or the breach thereof, shall be settled by arbitration through the services of Jay Folberg or anyone else on whom we mutually agree. Both parties agree to abide by any such arbitration decision.

A Joint Custody Agreement*

It is hereby stipulated by and between the parties, and approved by their counsel, that in the event the Court grants a divorce as prayed for in the Complaint, that the same shall be upon the following terms and conditions:

A. General Appearance and Proof of Complaint.

1. That defendant John C. Albert enters a general appearance in this action, consents to his default thereof and that plaintiff Virginia M. Albert may make proof in support of her Complaint on the merits.

B. Custody of the Minor Children.

2. That inasmuch as both parties desire and would ask the Court to grant them the care, custody and control of the minor children of the parties, and inasmuch as both parties recognize that each of them are fit and proper per-

---

*Reprinted with permission of attorney John C. Albert and of Virginia Albert.

sons to have the care, custody and control of the minor children, and inasmuch as both parties are agreeable to a joint custody arrangement under certain terms and conditions, and inasmuch as the parties have conferred with the office of Family Court Counseling as to the feasibility of such an arrangement and its terms and conditions and inasmuch as the office of Family Court Counseling has given its approval to a joint custody arrangement herein under certain terms and conditions, custody of the minor children of the parties shall be joint between the parties pursuant to the following terms and conditions.

(a) Specific days and times with a given parent shall be mutually worked out and agreed to by each party with a view toward providing continuity and predictability in their lives, and with a view toward the best interests of the minor children; that it is contemplated that actual physical custody of the minor children with each parent shall be fairly equal, considerations being given to the needs of the minor children and each parent; that the office of Family Court Counseling will avail itself and will assist the parties in setting up days and times that the minor children will be with a given parent.

(b) When any or both of the minor children is in the actual physical custody of a parent, that custodial parent shall have the responsibility for seeing to it that the minor children are fed properly, taken to a child sitter or taken to school, and that other and necessary needs of the minor children are met; that a parent having actual physical custody of any of the minor children shall at the time take responsibility for meeting medical and dental emergencies and that in emergencies the permission of both parents shall not be necessary.

(c) Each of the parties shall have occasion to take vacations away from home, and it is recognized that the vacationing parent may take the minor children along on vacations, keeping their best interests in view, or that the non-vacationing parent shall have the actual care and custody of the minor children when the other parent is on vacation.

(d) Both of the minor children shall have their legal residence in the same school district.

(e) Child care providers shall be mutually agreed to by

the parties and the parties shall share equally in the cost of child care providers.

(f)   John C. Albert shall maintain in full force and effect, comprehensive policies of health, medical, and dental insurance covering and naming the minor children as beneficiaries thereon; that health, medical, and dental costs and expenses not covered by insurance shall be shared equally by the parties.

(g)   The parties shall maintain in full force and effect the following policies of life insurance naming as irrevocable beneficiaries thereon the minor children of the parties at least until said children or any of them reach the age of eighteen (18).

(h)   Claims, causes of action, awards, rewards, or inheritances for or belonging to the minor children of the parties shall be handled as follows: any net recovery, award, reward or inheritance in excess of $5,000.00 shall be placed in trust for the benefit of the minor children of the parties; that sums not in excess of $5,000.00 may be expended but only for the benefit of the minor children of the parties.

(i)   The consent of both parties shall be required to effect the withdrawal of savings accounts for or belonging to the minor children of the parties.

(j)   If either party desires to remove herself/himself outside the Madison city limits, then the permission of the other party shall be sought; that should a dispute concerning the residence of a party arise, it is recognized that resolution may be sought through the office of Family Court Counseling, or through the determination and order of the Court.

(k)   Upon the remarriage of any of the parties, the present custody arrangement contemplated herein shall be subject to review.

(l)   Any disputes or disagreements regarding the terms and conditions of custody herein shall be initially taken to the office of Family Court Counseling for resolution and recommendation.

3.   It is recognized and agreed that the terms and conditions of the joint custody arrangement set forth above shall be supplemented or changed as the needs of the minor children change and/or as the best interests of the minor children may determine.

C. Child Support

4. As and for support of the minor children of the parties, John C. Albert shall pay the sum of $50.00 bi-weekly, such payments to be made to the Clerk of Courts of Dane County, by cash, cashier's check or bank money order, commencing

D. Child Dependency Tax Exemption

5. Each of the parties shall be entitled to claim one of the minor children as a dependent on his/her personal tax returns so long as permitted by law.

8

Special Problems and Issues

The joint custody agreement discussed in chapter 7 is developed by taking into account the needs and desires of the divorcing family at the time the divorce occurs. After families have lived with joint custody for some time, issues or problems that were not initially apparent may arise. As circumstances change, the original arrangement may in some cases require modification. Although it is not possible to predict all such potential changes, there are certain events which are likely to occur in joint custody families. Divorcing parents who realize that these special problems may arise will want to plan for their occurrence, and by doing so prevent them from causing serious difficulties.

REMARRIAGE

The remarriage of either parent is one special circumstance likely to arise in joint custody families. From a legal standpoint, if one or both parents want to remarry, the joint custody agreement does not have to be changed. However, in some of the agreements we reviewed, parents agreed at the time of divorce to return to court if either were to re-

111

marry. Inclusion of this clause reflects a recognition that remarriage will affect the joint custody arrangement.

One aspect of the joint custody agreement likely to be affected by the remarriage of either parent is the child's physical custody arrangement. Remarriage may result in either the parents or the child no longer being satisfied with the agreed-upon living arrangement. When some parents re-marry, they may wish to establish a more traditional family unit; they may feel that a joint custody arrangement in which the child alternates between homes interferes with this and may request that the child be permitted to spend more time with them. Obviously if issues like this arise, the parents will need to discuss the pros and cons of modifying the initial physical custody arrangement.

Children may also request a change in living arrangement following a parent's remarriage. Sometimes they become angry and jealous when a parent forms an important relationship with another adult. Seeing such a relationship grow may confuse or frighten some children, who may fear that they are in danger of losing the parent who remarries. For some this may result in their wanting to be near the remarried parent, while others may prefer to live with the parent who is still single. Although remarriage can present problems for any child, the shared physical custody of some joint custody arrangements may make these problems more pronounced.

The decision-making process of joint custody will also be affected by either remarriage or a parent's serious involvement with another adult. When others besides the original parents become involved, joint decision making becomes more complex. While it is often difficult for two adults to decide what is best for a child, it is likely to be much more so among two parents and one or two stepparents (or significant others). There is no easy way to handle this issue. Some might tell the stepparents to stay out of it, and let the parents decide; however, this response fails to acknowledge that since stepparents may have close contact with and responsibility for a child, they are very much affected by the decision-making process. Of course, stepparents are also important sources of support to their new spouses. For these reasons, it seems likely that at least on an informal level, stepparents or significant others will need to be included in the decision-making process.

These newcomers can help all family members adjust to their presence if they become involved slowly and cautiously in the joint custody arrangement. A stepparent who takes time to understand the formal and informal rules the joint custody family has developed and who tries to respect the rights of both parents will find that children and parents can better accept their influence on the arrangement than if they had rushed into judgments and advice. Those who immediately try to take a very active role in .the custody arrangement may be a disruptive force, and serious problems may result.

Since joint custody necessitates continued contact with an exspouse, divorced parents may also have ongoing contact with stepparents. For some this may be merely awkward, while for others it may be a constant source of pain. A parent who has had difficulty adjusting to a divorce may find such contact with a stepparent especially disconcerting.

A remarriage involving stepsiblings may further complicate the joint custody arrangement. Children who alternate between two homes may find it difficult to establish a good relationship with their new brothers or sisters. These youngsters may not understand why the joint custody children have a different routine than their own. If both parents remarry and there are stepsiblings in both families, the joint custody child may find it confusing that he or she has two sets of stepsiblings, but that neither set relates to each other.

When there are stepsiblings, joint custody decision making is an issue which must be handled carefully. As an example, let us take the issue of discipline or limit setting. If the joint custody parents have developed certain rules for a child, should these also apply to the stepsiblings? Do the rules or limits have to be the same? If they are not the same, what will be the effect of having different rules for different children who live in the same home? Will different rules make it more difficult for the joint custody child and the stepsiblings to establish a sense of family?

Remarriage is a probability for many divorcing parents, and there are no easy, standard answers to the problems that it may create for those with joint custody. Flexibility and a willingness to try to work out arrangements that will maximize the opportunities for all involved will insure an easier adjustment for the joint custody child, stepsiblings, stepparents, and parents themselves.

RELOCATION

Relocation, or moving, may not initially be a concern of divorcing parents. They are likely instead to be preoccupied with establishing a new home and lifestyle within the same locality. However, after a period of time, a divorced parent may begin to think seriously about moving. Perhaps a new job opportunity becomes available, or the parent decides that he or she needs more social contact than their locality permits.

This raises many issues for divorced parents, regardless of their custody arrangement. Those with joint custody face additional problems if one decides to make a major move. The magnitude of the changes that relocating may cause depends in part on the specifics of the joint custody arrangement. If the existing agreement involves regularly sharing the child's physical presence, any move that would not allow the boy or girl to remain in the same school district would require a modification in the custody arrangement. In such a case, perhaps the parents could agree to have the child live with one parent during the school year and the other during the summer.

Some parents may be able to work out an arrangement where both of them move to the same general location, which would allow the parents to maintain their joint custody arrangement. Before we began working on this book, we had a friend who shared custody. He decided that he wanted to move, but losing substantial contact with his children was unacceptable to him. After much discussion, he and his former wife found a new location acceptable to both of them; they have since moved and maintain their child-sharing arrangement. Although this will probably not be possible in many joint custody arrangements, it may be an alternative for some parents. More importantly, it illustrates the need for creativity and flexibility on the part of parents who are committed to maintaining a joint custody relationship.

For those who do not share physical custody of the children, the issue of moving may still be problematic. It is likely that the further one parent moves from the other, the more difficult it will be to regularly discuss matters related to the child. While certainly not impossible, joint decision making may become more costly, time-consuming, and difficult as the distance between parents increases.

A number of other changes may also interfere with an existing joint custody arrangement. For instance, a change in one parent's employment status or hours may necessitate modifying the custody agreement. Similarly, a significant change in the lifestyle of a parent may create either pragmatic or emotional problems for families who have joint custody.

As an example of how such a change could affect a joint custody family, assume that one parent becomes a devoted vegetarian; he or she decides that not eating meat is an appropriate, healthy lifestyle. Believing that this is important, the parent tries to convince the child not to eat meat—or perhaps no longer allows the child to eat such products in his or her home. The child may now find that a significant part of his or her life is spent in a place where meat is not permitted and a significant period of time where the failure to eat meat may bring punishment. The parents may begin to argue about which lifestyle is best for the children and how the conflicting habits will affect them. Although a similar situation could happen in any home, parents who live apart may be less likely to move toward a compromise of chosen habits. Because he or she maintains significant contact with both parents, the child may have difficulty living with these conflicts. Changes or modifications in religious beliefs, sexual preference, or any other major lifestyle can present problems for a joint custody family.

These families may also be confronted with societal problems. As we have discussed, many people may criticize or question those who decide on a joint custody arrangement. This response is undoubtedly related to the stigma which continues to surround divorce, as well as to the resistance to nontraditional childrearing roles.

Institutions or agencies may have difficulty adjusting to a joint custody family. This can be communicated to the family in several ways. Schools, for instance, may be confused about where to send report cards or whom to contact in case of an emergency. Teachers may be uncomfortable inviting both divorced parents to a parent-teacher conference. Similarly, hospital staffs may be in a quandary about whether they need to obtain both parent's signatures before treating a minor child. The problems that parents may encounter with institutions or agencies are similar to those experienced by a married woman who retains her maiden name. While certainly not overwhelming, such problems may become annoying.

Furthermore, problems that may only annoy a joint custody parent may be more serious for the child. The youngster will need to learn how to handle institutional responses to his or her living arrangement. Especially in the beginning, parents will need to anticipate problems and develop methods to prevent them. Perhaps they will decide that one address and phone number could be used on all "official" documents. The child should be aware of this, so that when at school the first day, he or she knows exactly what to put out on the line asking for an address. This is not as trivial as it may at first appear. It may be difficult enough for some children to adjust to their parent's divorce, without having to constantly explain their living arrangements. Think about how you would have felt as a child, standing in front of your class and saying that you didn't know how to fill out this card because you had two addresses. Your classmates would probably have responded with confusion —or worse, ridicule.

We have discussed some of the more common problems that may result as a family lives with its joint custody arrangement. Although there are no quick or definite solutions, one theme does recur. The joint custody family who anticipates situations will be in a position to develop preventive strategies. In doing so, they will minimize the likelihood of serious problems arising. Changes are inevitable in family relationships. A joint custody arrangement is more likely to be successful if divorcing parents are creative and flexible in dealing with these changes.

9

Interviews

Although each joint custody arrangement is unique, divorcing parents can learn a great deal from those who have lived with such custody. Until now, we have included only short quotations from family members to illustrate specific points about this form of custody. The interviews that follow provide a more detailed picture of how different parents and children have reacted to their experience with joint custody. We are indebted to these people for sharing their thoughts and feelings about this new alternative.

Anita K. Gold

Anita K. Gold is a thirty-five-year-old advertising executive. She was married to Arthur for seven years prior to their separation two years ago. They have one daughter, Ariana, who is now six years old. This was Arthur's second marriage; after his first he had joint custody of his son Jonathan. As she explains, Anita has had the unique experience of being both a stepparent in a joint custody agreement and having joint custody of her daughter.

MEL: How long have you and Arthur been separated?

ANITA: It's been almost two years now.

MEL: What type of separation arrangement have you had concerning the custody of your daughter Ariana?

ANITA: We've been following a joint custody arrangement which will be legal when our divorce is finalized. Ariana is with me one week and my husband one week.

MEL: How did you decide upon this arrangement?

ANITA: We had agreed on joint custody right from the beginning. It just became a question of working out the details.

MEL: Joint custody means different things to different people. What does it mean to you?

ANITA: Equal sharing and equal responsibility as close and equal as possible. It doesn't have to be absolutely fifty-fifty.

MEL: How did you know about joint custody—how did you find out about it?

ANITA: My husband had been married before, and he had joint custody of his son Jonathan, who is now nineteen years old. We started to go out together when Jonathan was eight years old and got married when he was eleven. So I was a stepparent in a joint custody arrangement for seven years.

MEL: What was it like being a stepparent to a joint custody child?

ANITA: A lot better for me than being a full parent. I didn't want to be a parent when I first got married. I like Jonathan, but I didn't marry with the idea of becoming a parent to someone else's child. I might have—but that wasn't in my mind at the time. The joint custody arrangement allowed Jonathan and I to become friends. We're still friends today.

MEL: When Jonathan was growing up, did you play an active role in his upbringing?

ANITA: Yes. For instance, I became very involved in his education. When he decided to go to college, we travelled around together looking at different schools. Essentially, I think I was the person most involved with Jonathan's education.

MEL: Since you were active in Jonathan's upbringing, how did you get along with his mother?

ANITA: That's interesting, I think. We became very friendly. In some ways joint custody created a large extended family situation. My daughter Ariana not only considers Jonathan as her brother, but also feels like Jonathan's other half sister is her sister. Although Ariana always seemed to understand all the different relationships, in some ways she felt like we were all one big family.

MEL: How do you think the joint custody arrangement worked for Jonathan?

ANITA: I think it was good for him. We have discussed it with him a number of times, and he indicated that overall he thought it was a positive experience. It's because he thought it was positive, and I felt it worked well, that my husband and I want joint custody of our daughter Ariana.

MEL: What benefits do you see for yourself that makes you want to have joint custody?

ANITA: In the beginning I wanted it theoretically, but not in actuality. It was difficult for me to go to sleep at night knowing Ariana wasn't there. I really missed her. As I got adjusted to that, I realized that joint custody has a lot of advantages for me. I wanted to go out and do things. Also, I travel occasionally when I work. Now I try to plan my trips when she's with her father. I know I'm leaving her with someone with whom she's physically and emotionally comfortable. Joint custody gives me a lot of freedom I wouldn't have had with sole custody.

MEL: Why do you think your exhusband wants joint custody? What are the benefits for him?

ANITA: He loves Ariana and wants to be a "real father." I feel very strongly about joint custody. I've met many men who are fathers without children. Sure they have visiting rights, but it's not the same thing. They are not full participants in their child's life. Some of them become "court jesters"; they think, "How shall I entertain my child this weekend?" And entertaining isn't really what parenting is all about.

MEL: How do you think Ariana feels about the joint custody arrangement?

ANITA: That's a difficult question to answer and one that everyone always asks. My exhusband and I think she's doing well, but with young kids it's difficult to know what reaction results from what. They go through so many stages, it's just difficult to tell.

MEL: We've talked about some of the positive aspects of joint custody; what do you see as the problems with joint custody?

ANITA: For one thing, there's the need to continue regular contact with my exhusband. Sometimes it seems like I deal with him as much now as when we were married. "Ariana seems upset lately; did you notice it?" "Did you study with her this week?" "She has to go to the doctor: will you take her or shall I?" I know that in some joint custody relationships parents just drop their kids off and pick them up, but I think it's important to know what's going on on both sides.

MEL: How about other problems?

ANITA: There are day-to-day problems. Probably one of the biggest is, where is her stuff? Her books, sneakers, clothes, bike, etc. We have two sets of some things, but we can't afford two of everything. It becomes difficult moving things back and forth, back and forth, but that's one of the realities of this arrangement. Also, schools and institutions aren't really accustomed to joint custody and don't know how to deal with it. Last summer we had a real problem with a day camp. We couldn't get the day camp to give Ariana a place on two buses, even though we were willing to pay the extra bus cost. It turned out that a place on the bus meant a place in camp, so we would have had to pay the full camp cost for two children. We had to send her by cab, and that cost quite a lot of money.

MEL: Joint custody involves joint decision making. How do you and your exhusband make decisions which concern Ariana?

ANITA: We make major decisions together. Since we share financial responsibility, it's even more important that we agree on decisions, as they often involve money. Generally decision making hasn't been a problem. We're pretty compatible about our beliefs and both want what's best for our daughter.

MEL: Is there anything else you can tell me about your joint custody arrangement?

ANITA: I should tell you a little bit more about the way we work it, since I'm sure it's unusual. We have a housekeeper that moves with our daughter. For us this is a necessity. My exhusband and I both have jobs that at times necessitate our working long hours. We had a housekeeper when we were married and decided to continue this. It works out well, since Ariana likes her and feels an extra sense of stability and continuity.

MEL: Are there any issues that aren't problematic now, but that may arise in the future concerning joint custody?

ANITA: One thing that concerns me is remarriage. I visit my daughter twice a week when she is at her father's house. I wonder what will happen if he remarries. How would another woman feel about having me there, and how would I feel?

MEL: Is there a reason you have to visit at his house?

ANITA: I don't want to go a whole week without seeing her. I could take her out for dinner, but that becomes entertaining. And it means depriving him on those evenings. I would like to avoid it.

MEL: Any last comments about joint custody?

ANITA: Just that I think it has the potential to work out well for everyone involved, but it also takes a lot of work to make it successful.

TOM JOHNSON AND LINDA BECK

Tom was married for seven years prior to his divorce three years ago. He has joint custody of his daughter Sarah. Although in most cases joint custody results in significant contact between divorcing parents, in the following interview Tom discusses how and why he has maintained a great deal of separation from his exwife. Linda, who presently lives with Tom, also takes part in the interview.

MEL: Why did you want joint custody of your daughter?

TOM: Initially, it was because I didn't feel I could get sole custody. I think my exwife felt the same way. Joint custody also seems like a natural continuation of the custody you have in marriage. It just continues the process, so no one person goes to zero and no one goes to 100 percent.

MEL: You say it continues the process. When you were married, did you play a big role in bringing up your daughter?

TOM: Yes. I spent a lot of time with Sarah when she was very young. The flexibility of my job and my exwife being in school contributed to this. But I definitely played a large role in her early upbringing.

MEL: When I first called to ask if you would be willing to talk about your custody arrangement, you said that you had some problems with joint custody. What are they?

TOM: My exwife and I had different conceptions of what joint custody meant and how it should work. For me, joint custody meant that each parent could individually continue to have a relationship with their child. For some other people, including my exwife, joint custody meant that you continue to raise the child together even though you live apart. To me that seems odd. We have different styles that we can't bring together. I realized that for some people joint custody means working together—cooperation and togetherness. That takes a lot of time and work, and I feel I would be better off using that effort here, with my daughter.

LINDA: It was difficult to achieve this separateness. We were in the position of saying to Tom's exwife and her husband: "We don't want to join you, do things together, or be your friends." That's hard to say to someone.

TOM: It was the only way I could work it. Sharing the child doesn't have to mean that the two parents continue a relationship. My exwife expected to have almost a camaraderie. For me that wasn't a possibility.

LINDA: I think it would be difficult for the child to be in a place with four adults who are all authority figures to her. That's likely to be confusing, so I think the separateness is a good thing.

TOM: It's a good thing, but it's also very strange. In this culture there really is no right way to deal with these new relationships. There are no cultural models.

MEL: How does your daughter seem to be doing in your joint custody arrangement?

TOM: She seems to be doing very well. There really haven't been any major problems. I think she likes the regular contact she has with both me and my exwife. She gets a lot of affection from both places. I worry about her, but she seems to be doing fine.

MEL: What benefits do you think joint custody provides for your daughter?

TOM: First, like I said before, she still has two parents to relate to. Also, since we have somewhat different life-styles, values, and beliefs, seeing these may give her some independence from both of them. When she gets older, she'll be in a better position to choose how she wants to live her life.

MEL: Since you've chosen to maintain a great deal of separation from your exwife, how do you make decisions about Sarah?

TOM: When we first started with joint custody, we had a flexible physical custody arrangement. This made it necessary to have a lot of contact with each other, to decide on day-to-day things. Now that we have a more routine physical arrangement, we really don't need to be in very much contact. Often we communicate through Sarah. Of course, there are times we do need to make decisions. Then we call or sometimes write letters.

MEL: How often do you actually speak to your exwife?

TOM: No more than once a month, and often less. I'm sure part of it is related to the kind of person I am. People need to work out an arrangement which reflects who they are. I didn't see the need for or want a lot of contact.

MEL: My guess is that some people who read this will wonder how your daughter can do well living in two homes where there are differing values, with parents who rarely communicate with each other.

LINDA: We feel certain that she's loved as much in her other home as she is here. That's really important. She loves both her parents, and they love her.

TOM: That's right. I don't see joint custody, no matter how the couple work it out, as purely good or purely bad. It's hard to tell in advance what it's going to do to your life or your child's life. I think both my exwife and I really care about our daughter, and so far the arrangement has worked out well. For me, the separateness was the only way it had any chance of working.

CAROL AND CHARLES DYNER

Carol and Charles Dyner have been divorced for more than a year after being separated for eighteen months. They have one son, Karl, who is twelve years old.

Following their divorce Carol was granted sole custody of Karl. Soon afterward, however, the Dyners decided to try a joint custody type arrangement which involved Karl living with one of them every other week. Recently Karl told his parents that he was not happy with the living arrangement. In the following interview, we discuss the Dyners' informal joint custody arrangement and the specific problem Karl had with the physical living situation.

MEL: Why did you decide to try a joint custody arrangement after you had been living with a sole custody arrangement for some time?

CAROL: As I recall, it was Charles who first wanted it.

CHARLES: Right. Actually it wasn't anything that I had ever really heard about. I simply wanted to have more contact with my son, to continue and improve our relationship. I wasn't at that time thinking of a legal or socioeconomic concept; I simply wanted to be more of a parent to Karl.

MEL: How did that sound to you?

CAROL: I felt good about it—it was fine with me.

MEL: You started a joint custody type arrangement fourteen months after your separation. Could you have started it right away?

CHARLES: I don't think there was any way we could have started then. We weren't in communication with each other. I personally wasn't ready for that then.

CAROL: Neither was I. The summer Charles left was a nightmare for all of us. Karl and I hung on like two people on a raft. It was a shock to both of us. I remember how I wanted to smother Karl and protect him. On the other hand, I knew that was wrong. Charles left on July 4, and Karl went right to day camp. It was a new day camp, and he'd never been there before—but he went. That's not easy for a kid who's been shocked. But Karl went to camp that summer, and we all lived through the separation. We needed time for us all to calm down. But after awhile, when Charles suggested that we share custody, I was ready and willing to try and see if it could work.

CHARLES: We asked Karl, and he was agreeable. So he started to spend one week with me and one week with Carol. This has been going on for six months. However, only a few days ago, Karl told us that he didn't want to continue alternating every other week.

MEL: Karl, can you tell me what you haven't liked about the situation?

KARL: Well, it was confusing. I'd go to sleep, wake up, and not know exactly where I was. I didn't know if I was at my mother's or my father's apartment.

MEL: So it was confusing?

KARL: Yeah, I just thought maybe I'd lay off the joint custody for awhile. (Everybody laughs.)

CAROL: Karl, you also said that there were problems with Daddy's apartment.

KARL: Over at my father's apartment I don't have my own room. I just sleep there. He has some games and stuff, but most of my posters and games aren't there. Sometimes I'll say, "Hey, let's play this real neat game," and then I remember it's in my closet at the other apartment.

CHARLES: Recently I was going to get a two-bedroom apartment so that Karl could have his own room. When I told Karl about this, I think he was afraid that if I changed apartments and he didn't want to stay with me, that it would hurt my feelings, cost extra money, and things.

CAROL: I think that's right. When Karl told me he wanted to go back to the way things were before, he cried and said, "I'm going to hurt Daddy. I'm going to hurt his feelings."

KARL: Now that it's out, maybe I'll want to try it again sometime. I've got lots of years ahead of me. I think it was that weird dream I had that made me realize I didn't like the living arrangement.

MEL: What dream was that?

KARL: I dreamt that my mother had died. She was trapped from me. I was on a bus, and the driver was driving away from the stop. My mother was pounding on the door, trying to get in. I said, "Come on, let me out," but the guy wouldn't open the door. I saw my mother drop. When I finally got off the bus a few blocks away, I ran—and when I got to her, someone said she's dead.

MEL: You must have been really scared.

KARL: I was. When I woke up, I realized that I didn't know where I was. I wanted to call my mother.

CAROL: Right after that, all the things about confusion and wanting to go back to the way it was before came out.

MEL: Karl, were there any other problems you had with the joint custody arrangement?

KARL: Not usually. School was a little problem. I had to get a bus pass, since when I'm at my father's apartment I have to take a bus to school. Everybody would ask me, "Why do you need a bus pass when you live just across the street?" I had to get my parents to sign something saying I legally lived with my father, so I could get the bus pass. That was really the only other problem.

MEL: Now that these problems have come up, what are you going to do?

CHARLES: We've decided to go back to the way it was before. Karl will live primarily with Carol and spend one night each week with me. Karl knows that if he changes his mind or wants to spend a few extra days with me, he can. We both want to do what's best for Karl, and right now it seems clear that alternating each week isn't working out, so we'll change.

MEL: Will you continue to try to make decisions about Karl together?

CAROL: Definitely.

CHARLES: I know that Carol, because she has legal custody, has more legal say in making decisions which affect Karl. But I think that both our concerns about him are equal, and I don't fear she'll do something rash without consulting me.

CAROL: We basically have the same ideas about raising children, so I don't think making joint decisions will be a real problem.

MEL: It sounds like you are going to try to continue a joint custody type arrangement with Karl living primarily with Carol.

CHARLES AND CAROL: That's right.

JONATHAN SPENCER PEARLSROTH

In the first interview Anita K. Gold referred to her stepson, Jonathan. We later had the opportunity to speak with

him. Jonathan Spencer Pearlsroth is a nineteen-year-old college student. There are few adults who can reflect on their
childhood experiences with joint custody, so we feel fortu-
nate to have been able to speak with Jonathan, a young man
who has lived with such an arrangement for the past sixteen years.

MEL: Jonathan, you lived in a joint custody arrangement
            for most of your life?
JONATHAN: That's right. My parents got a divorce when I was
            three years old, and I began to alternately live with
            each of them. Actually, for awhile I lived primarily
            with my mother and visited my father, but after he
            got an apartment with a separate bedroom I began
            to spend more time with him. I think it worked out
            that I spent 70 percent of the time with my mother
            and 30 percent with my father.
MEL: Did you feel different from other kids because of
            your living situation?
JONATHAN: I think I felt different because my parents were di-
            vorced, not because of the living arrangement. It took
            some time before I realized that there were a lot of
            kids from divorced families.
MEL: How did you feel about alternating between your
            parents' apartments?
JONATHAN: At first it was strange. I didn't understand why they
            were separated, and I didn't like moving back and
            forth between apartments. Sometimes I'd even pre-
            tend I was sick so that I wouldn't have to move.
MEL: What were the problems with moving between the
            apartments?
JONATHAN: It was inconvenient. Sometimes I just didn't feel like
            packing up my things and going to the other apart-
            ment. It got to be a hassle—even though my parents
            only lived ten blocks from each other. I would spend
            one day with my father, two days with my mother,
            and so on. I moved quite a bit.
MEL: Did you continue to be dissatisfied with your living
            arrangement?
JONATHAN: No. I think I felt that way from about the time I was
            three until about eight, from nine to twelve or thir-

teen I really didn't care one way or the other. And then, when I got to be about thirteen years old, it dawned on me that there really were advantages to joint custody.

MEL: What were they?

JONATHAN: I got to see both my parents regularly. In reality, I suppose that meant seeing my father more often. I had several friends whose parents were divorced, and they only saw their fathers infrequently. Since mothers usually had custody, I felt lucky about my situation, lucky that I was able to spend a lot of time with both of my parents.

MEL: Were there other advantages?

JONATHAN: Definitely. I have a really large family. I have two parents, two stepparents, two sisters and eight grandparents. These people are all close to me, and I'm glad I have the chance to know all of them.

MEL: Are your two sisters from your "new" families?

JONATHAN: Yes. Technically they're my stepsisters, but I think of them as sisters. The two of them get along so well that they think of each other as sisters even though they're not related. In some ways a similar thing happened with my parents and stepparents. Although, at first, there was a good deal of bickering, slowly they all began to relate to each other in a friendly, almost familial way.

MEL: One component of this form of custody is joint decision making. How did your parents make decisions which affected you?

JONATHAN: I think they made most of the big decisions together. I remember when I wanted to go to summer camp they both thought about it, and we all discussed it. Most of the time they split my expenses, so I guess it was important that they made decisions together.

MEL: How did you think joint decision making worked out?

JONATHAN: There were some arguments. But when I look back at it now they were mostly related to their divorce, not me. I think they both had similar beliefs about raising me. They were very conscientious parents.

MEL: When you wanted to do something, or you needed something, which parent did you ask?

JONATHAN: Usually I would ask whichever parent I was with at the time. Occasionally I'd think, "Who is the most lenient parent?" and ask that one. This didn't work very often if it was an important issue because one or the other would say, "It's okay with me, but you'll have to clear it with your mother or father."

MEL: Some people say that joint custody traps a child in the middle, between both parents. Did you ever feel this way?

JONATHAN: Once in a while that happened. I can remember my father saying, "Who do you love?" I don't think my parents meant to put me in the middle, but sometimes it happened. It was a good feeling too though—knowing that both my parents were trying to win me over.

MEL: Getting back to your living arrangement, you said there were some problems—were changes made to make it more satisfying?

JONATHAN: When I was fourteen the schedule, or when I would stay where, was more and more left up to me. My parents were flexible and it worked out well. If I was doing something special or really didn't feel like switching places, I could stay longer periods of time with either parent.

MEL: As a kind of summary, what do you think about joint custody? What advice do you have for divorcing families?

JONATHAN: I think it's really the only way to settle the child issue in divorce. If both parents express a desire to be involved with their child, even though there is no longer a tight-knit family, then joint custody is the answer. Although it was tough for me in the beginning, I think it would have been even harder if all of a sudden I had hardly any contact with my mother or father. I really want to emphasize that I think the best way to raise a child is for both parents to be involved. I really enjoyed spending time with both my parents, and in fact, I still do.

10

Joint Custody Research

Increasing amounts of information on joint custody can be found in magazines and newspapers. While these articles provide parents and professionals with a better understanding of this new custody alternative, they are for the most part not substantiated by solid evidence or research. This reflects the current level of awareness and knowledge about joint custody. There is simply not a great deal known about the effects of joint custody on mothers, fathers, or children.

Researchers have only recently begun to study such families, and some of the most relevant research has just recently been published. In the future this work and further studies may become accessible to parents and professionals. In this chapter we will review the research which has been done in the area of joint custody. It provides information and insight into the experiences of families who have chosen to live with this custody arrangement. Conclusions from four studies of families who have legal joint custody or joint custody type arrangements and two studies on the involvement of divorced fathers with their children will be discussed.

One of the authors of this book, Nadine Nehls, studied a small group of divorced parents who were awarded joint custody of their children. Twelve parents, representing eight families, responded to a mail questionnaire intended to elicit information about several major issues on the subject.

MEANS OF INTRODUCTION TO JOINT CUSTODY

Because joint custody is a relatively new and controversial custody option, parents often need to actively seek out information and advice in learning about it. Questions were asked to ascertain how these joint custody families found out about this alternative to sole custody.

The findings were very interesting. The largest percentage of parents said that joint custody was their own idea. As might be expected, the majority of them sought out further information between the time that they first considered joint custody and being granted it by the court. The most common sources of additional information for women were a lawyer, family court counselor, or a printed source. The men most frequently consulted with a court counselor.

CHARACTERISTICS OF JOINT CUSTODY FAMILIES

Some people have hypothesized that parents who have joint custody are likely to be from higher socioeconomic groups. This proved to be true in this study; most parents who participated in it earned from $15,000 to $19,000 yearly, an income above normal for this particular geographic area. The parents were also highly educated; eight out of twelve had completed at least one year of graduate study.

Probably the two most unique and controversial aspects of joint custody concern the child's living arrangement and the equal rights and responsibilities of divorced parents. In the study parents were asked questions about these two areas.

Living Arrangement

In three of the eight families represented in this study, physical custody of the child was shared equally. In an equal number of families, the child or children spent more than half of their time in the home of one parent. The remaining two families had an arrangement typically referred to as "split custody"; that is, one or more of their children lived primarily with one parent, while one or more lived primarily with the other parent. The table below summarizes the physical living arrangements of these eight families.

Table 10–1

Summary of Children's Physical Living Situation by Family

Family N = 8	Child or Children's Living Situation
1	Live (s) primarily with mother.
2	Live (s) primarily with father.*
3	Some of the children live with father, some live with mother; all alternate on weekends.
4	Some of the children live with father, some live with mother.
5	Live (s) with father one week, mother the next.
6	Live (s) with father Sunday-Friday, with mother on weekends.
7	Live (s) with mother Sunday-Wednesday, with father Wednesday-Saturday.
8	Live (s) with mother two days, then with father two days; alternate (s) each weekend.

*The mother noted that this was a temporary arrangement.

Decision Making

Parents were asked to specify how they made decisions about six aspects of childrearing: education, religion, health, discipline, limit-setting, and finances. Most stated that decisions regarding these areas were made jointly. Interestingly, discipline and limit-setting were singled out by several parents as areas where decisions were not made together but rather by whichever parent had physical custody of the child. This supports the assumption that in joint custody families major decisions are often made jointly, while day-to-day decisions are made by the parent who is with the child at the time.

While respondees did not think that joint decision making was difficult for children, they felt differently about the effect of joint decision making on parents. Nine out of twelve parents strongly agreed that joint decision making is difficult for parents.

CHILD SATISFACTION

The effects of joint custody on children were an important focus of this study. In general, the responding parents perceived their children to be satisfied with the custody arrangement. Of the twelve children in these eight families, five were perceived by their parents to be "very satisfied" with joint custody, six "fairly satisfied," and one "somewhat satisfied-somewhat dissatisfied."

All but one parent felt there were advantages to joint custody which their children would not have with sole custody. In a majority of cases, both mothers and fathers considered that the most important advantage of joint custody was that both parents maintained an active and/or meaningful role in the child's life.

According to their parents' perceptions, nine out of the twelve children were experiencing only minor problems with joint custody. Parents felt that the most difficult problems concerned children living alternately with each parent. More specifically, they cited problems in adjusting to two different houses and lifestyles, confusion about rules, and separation from favorite friends. However, it is interesting that of those answering this question, two of the four families had an arrangement where the child's time was equally divided between two homes, while in the other two the children lived primarily with one parent. Thus, neither the amount of time spent in each home nor the frequency of transition between them appears to be the crucial variable of this problem. Perhaps the adjustment to two different homes, lifestyles, and sets of rules is no more problematic for a child of joint custody than for one whose parents have sole custody with significant visitation.

PARENTAL SATISFACTION

Another major objective of this study was to determine whether parents were satisfied with their joint custody arrangements. In general, those who participated rated their personal satisfaction with joint custody quite favorably. Five of the seven fathers and two of the four mothers stated that they were "very satisfied" with the arrangement; the remaining mothers were "fairly satisfied," while the remaining fathers reported feeling "somewhat satisfied-somewhat dissatisfied." None of the parents stated that they were "dissatisfied" with joint custody. Perhaps most significantly, eight of the twelve parents said that if they had to do it over again they would choose joint custody over sole custody. While four were unsure, no one reported that they would definitely choose sole custody.

The reasons for parental satisfaction may be better understood if we look at the advantages and disadvantages of joint custody reported by these parents. The most important advantage reported by women was sharing responsibility for the child or children. This included such things as expenses, decision making, and actual care of the child. Men most often cited the opportunity for the child to maintain contact with both parents as the most important advantage.

A majority of the parents reported that joint custody had presented them with minor problems. However, no single problem stood out. The problems included adjusting to the child's absence, explaining joint custody to children, financial concerns, reaching mutually agreeable decisions, scheduling other events around the joint custody arrangement, and dealing with the child's loss of routine after time spent with the other parent. Unlike the situation for children, there does not appear to be a predominate issue which was problematic for these mothers or fathers.

SUMMARY

In general, the results of this study substantiate the feasibility of joint custody arrangements. The results reveal that these parents are generally satisfied with their custody arrangement. Contrary to popular opinion, joint custody has not presented these mothers, fathers, or children with serious problems; instead a majority of the parents cited distinct advantages for themselves and their children which they would not have had with sole custody. Other studies have reached similar conclusions about this form of custody.

Dr. Alice Abarbanel completed a doctoral dissertation on joint custody families at the California School of Professional Psychology. Using an intensive case study approach, Dr. Abarbanel studied four families who were living with joint custody arrangements. For this study, families were defined as having joint custody if the parental division of child-care responsibility ranged from 50/50 to 67/33 and the children lived with one parent or the other no longer than two weeks at a time.

The results of this study suggest that joint custody offers both advantages and disadvantages to children and parents. Dr. Abarbanel concludes: "It [joint custody] is neither 'good' nor 'bad'; it works under certain conditions" (Abarbanel, 1979, p. 328). She goes on to explain, "There is no doubt that joint custody yields two psychological parents, and that the children do not suffer the profound sense of loss characteristic of so many children of divorce. The children maintained strong attachments to both parents. Perhaps, the security of an ongoing relationship with *two* psychological parents helps to provide the means to cope successfully with the uprooting effects of switching households (Abarbanel, 1979, p. 328).

Susan Shavin, another student at the California School of Professional Psychology, also studied joint custody families. Although the results of her master's thesis are not published, several interesting findings are reported in *The Disposable Parent—The Case for Joint Custody* (Roman and Haddad, 1978). Shavin did not find, as some have, that joint custody families were of a particular socio-economic group. But as is expected, the seventeen families she studied had very different physical custody arrangements, varying from families who alternated physical custody within each week to families who alternated physical custody each year.

Mel Roman and his colleagues at Albert Einstein College of Medicine have also been studying joint custody families. In their book, Roman and Haddad present three case studies of joint custody families which also demonstrate the diversity and dynamics of families who choose this custody option.

Dr. Constance Ahrons, of the University of Wisconsin-Madison, has studied co-parenting relationships following divorce (1979, 1980). One aspect of her research deals with divorced parents who have been awarded joint custody in the San Diego area. Dr. Ahrons explains that in San Diego County physical custody is a separate decision which is specified within the joint custody agreement. Upon awarding joint custody, the court may decide to award physical custody to either the mother or father, to both parents on an alternating basis, or to divide the custody of the children between them.

Ahrons (1980) found that "the majority of divorced parents in this study (84%) reported that overall they were satisfied with their joint custody arrangement. The major reasons they gave for this satisfaction clustered into two categories: 1) having access to both parents was better for their children; and 2) the joint custody arrangement permitted more flexibility for child care." (p. 192)

In regard to decision making, these joint custody parents most frequently shared in "making major decisions regarding children's lives, discussing school and/or medical problems, and planning special events" (1980, p. 196). Parents were less likely to share in making day-to-day decisions about the children. "Although some parents did divide parenting responsibilities fairly equally, the majority were involved in a variety of shared parenting patterns, with differential involvement of the nonresidential [parent without physical custody] parents" (1980, p. 201). Consequently, Ahrons (1980) points out "that 'joint' did not necessarily mean 'equal'" (p. 201).

Until recently the divorced father has received little attention. Two new studies, however, have focused on divorcing fathers and are particularly relevant to the subject of joint custody.

Dr. Judith Brown Grief has done research on this subject at Albert Einstein College. Her doctoral dissertation explored fathers' perceptions of their relationships with children following separation and divorce. Of the sixty-three parent-child relationships examined in this study, eighty percent of the children were in custody of their mothers; the others were in joint custody of both parents.

She discovered that many fathers suffered emotional and physical reactions due to the feeling of loss and the decreased contact with their child. However, "the greater the father's involvement with his child, the greater his sense of having an ongoing parental role in the child's life after divorce. Most importantly, this becomes self-reinforcing: the more opportunity fathers have to act as fathers, the more they see themselves as fathers and seek to continue that involvement. Similarly, those fathers who had more contact with, and joint custody of, their children were significantly more satisfied than fathers with less contact and no custodial rights" (Grief, 1979, p. 313).

Harry Finkelstein Keshet and Kristine M. Rosenthal have also studied divorced fathers. These researchers looked at four groups: those with their children full-time; those with their children half-time; those with their children quarter-time; and those with their children once in a while. Their conclusion was that fathers who had their children half of the time were the happiest. "Half-time fathers seem the most comfortable in child care . . . had the least conflict with their former wives . . . and . . . were most satisfied with their living arrangements" (*Human Behavior,* November 1978. p. 37).

The results of these studies, while based on relatively small samples, lend weight to the case that there are indeed potential benefits of joint custody for divorcing families. Certainly joint custody is not a panacea for all such families, but for some it may serve to abate the potential adverse effects of divorce and sole custody. Such studies suggest that this form of custody may indeed be the best practical means of satisfying the psychosocial needs of some women, men, and children following divorce.

11

Is It for Your Family?

The divorcing parent who nears the conclusion of this book has probably been asking himself or herself whether or not to try joint custody. Similarly, people reading it who live in sole custody arrangements may wonder whether joint custody would have worked better for them and whether there are ways to make their sole custody situation more like joint custody. Professionals in the legal and mental health areas who work with divorcing families may be considering to whom they might suggest exploring this option.

If one thing stands out in our discussion of joint custody, it is that there are no easy answers to the custody question. Custody options have been manifestations of the social and economic realities of the historical periods when they occurred. The swinging of a pendulum provides an appropriate visual image of custody decision making in the past; what was seen as the right and appropriate custody decision in the eighteenth and early nineteenth centuries in the United States seemed wrong or inappropriate in the early twentieth century. Today the pendulum has come to rest in the middle, somewhere between father preference and mother preference. This middle position seems represented by joint custody, a custody arrangement that recognizes both mothers' and fathers' contribution to parenting.

Constantly changing attitudes toward custody indicate that there is probably no totally right nor consistently wrong custody option. The needs and wishes of specific families at specific times govern what is the best custody arrangement for a particular family.

The best that anyone can offer a divorcing family is information about all possible custody options and suggestions about how to reach a decision. Advisers can only provide the parameters, the boundaries, within which a family can operate. Some of these are set by the courts and vary from locality to locality. Other boundaries are offered by professionals knowledgeable about family relations and child growth and development.

We have attempted to offer guidelines, suggestions, ideas, and facts about joint custody, hoping that this will increase the options available to divorcing parents. We conclude by presenting a list of important questions that divorcing parents will need to think about when considering this custody alternative. These questions are intended to highlight the issues already discussed and to put parents in touch with their feelings about custody in general and joint custody in specific.

WHY AM I CONSIDERING JOINT CUSTODY?

This is one of the most crucial questions a divorcing parent must ask. The answer will help the parent to better understand his or her motivation for desiring this custody arrangement. Responses to this question will probably fall into three main categories:

1. I believe that joint custody is in the best interests of all involved.
2. I want sole custody, but am afraid I won't get it, so I'll settle for joint custody.

3. I feel like I should want at least joint custody; if I don't, it must mean I don't love my child.

Obviously, the answer which seems to be the most appropriate motivation for pursuing joint custody is number one. If you honestly believe that a joint custody arrangement is in everyone's best interests, you are well on your way to success with it. By "all involved" we mean that the divorcing parent has considered the needs of the children, and of his or her former spouse, as well as his or her own needs.

Some parents may feel pressure to pursue a joint custody arrangement because—as suggested in this book and elsewhere—joint custody may be in the best interests of the child. However, we want to reemphasize that a child only benefits when parents want and are willing to cooperate with a joint custody arrangement. If either or both parents definitely do not want such custody, it will not be in the child's best interests. The ideal motivation for considering this form of custody is a belief that it will best meet the needs of the children *and* the parents, coupled with a willingness on the part of both the mother and father to make joint custody successful.

It is more difficult to ascertain whether the second response above will lead to success. In some cases, a divorcing parent may truly want sole custody but feel—perhaps on the advice of an attorney—that he or she is unlikely to be awarded it. We have noted that men who have wanted sole custody have traditionally had to convince the court that the mother was unfit. While this is not always the case today, some men are still discouraged from seeking custody of their children, and professionals and friends may infer that it isn't worth the fight. Similarly, some mothers might feel that due to their particular circumstances, or to the extraordinary fitness of their husbands, they may be denied sole custody by the court. In such cases, a parent might decide that it is better to pursue joint custody than to risk losing sole custody of the child. The likelihood of this motivation resulting in a successful joint custody arrangement depends to a great extent on the relationship between the divorcing parents. If they can honestly work together to pursue joint custody rather than threaten each other with a custody fight, the arrangement may prove to be a positive experience for all involved. In fact, once parents accept the notion that both want and have a right to be involved in their child's life, they are often better able to recognize the potential benefits of a joint custody arrangement. However, if the parents do not trust each other or are unable to accept their mutual involvement in the child's life and thus cannot work together on common goals, there is little chance of joint custody achieving its purposes. Stated another way, if one or both parents really wants sole custody and this desire interferes with their ability to cooperate on issues related to their child, then a joint custody arrangement will not be in the family's best interests.

The third response to the question of motivation can be the most problematic. As joint custody becomes more common and acceptable, divorcing parents may increasingly feel pressured to request this custody option. For decades, women have been told by society that they should want custody of their child; those who have decided otherwise have been chastised. The option of joint custody could result in an analogous type of pressure on both mothers and fathers. Initially this will be especially true for men; fathers who have for years been taught that they should not want custody may feel pressure to conform to a growing trend toward shared custodial arrangements. In this way joint custody has the potential to become another "guilt trip." It is difficult to ignore society's "shoulds," the overt and subtle encouragements to aspire to common mandates and goals. However, divorcing parents who choose a joint custody arrangement only because they are told that they should want to do so will probably have a difficult time making it work. It would be extremely unfortunate if joint custody became a fad which people felt obliged to try.

Custodial arrangements can have profound effects on everyone involved; consequently, the issue of custody is an extremely important decision which should not be based on trends or whims. We hope that this will never become the case with joint custody. Thinking and writing about this alternative is exciting because it increases the options available to divorcing families by challenging myths regarding traditional custody decision making. However, if new myths merely replace the old, it will only result in a new "custody trap" for parents and children. Susan Whicher, head of the American Bar Association's special committee on joint custody is of the opinion that by the end of the 1980s, joint custody will be the rule rather than the exception (*Time,* 1979). While the increase in joint custody arrangements may not be quite this pronounced, we hope that its growth will stem from a positive and healthy motivation of parents rather than from feelings of guilt and obligation.

After parents have examined their motivation for wanting joint custody, answers to a number of other questions will help to clarify its potential for success. Answering "yes" to all of the questions listed below will not guarantee a successful joint custody arrangement, nor does a "no" answer mean that the arrangement will not work. However, a parent who answers "no" to any of the questions below should carefully consider the feasibility of joint custody in his or her particular case. The questions are intended to summarize factors which we believe contribute to the success of joint custody.

1. Do I think that my former spouse is a good parent?
2. Do I believe that the type of joint custody arrangement I want allows for the stability and consistency necessary for our child?
3. Am I able and willing to discuss matters related to our child with my former spouse?

4. Do my former spouse and I have compatible beliefs about raising children?
5. Am I willing to ask for help in settling major differences that might arise between my former spouse and I concerning our child?
6. As circumstances change, am I willing to make adjustments in our joint custody arrangement to maximize the potential for its success?

As we were finishing this book we thought, Wouldn't it be helpful if we could refer to an "ideal" joint custody family with whom most of our readers would be familiar? Although we do not mean to imply that an "ideal" joint custody family exists, a recent popular movie does provide an excellent opportunity to imagine a situation in which joint custody might be the preferred custody option. We are talking, of course, about the Academy Award winning picture, Kramer vs. Kramer. The film starred Dustin Hoffman and Meryl Streep as divorcing parents who fight over custody of their son, Justin Henry. When the couple initially separates Meryl Streep leaves the son with his father. She returns later and wants custody. At this point in the film, we see a couple for whom joint custody does not seem workable. Hoffman and Streep are both extremely angry and hostile over the circumstances surrounding their separation and divorce. They show little respect for each other, do not communicate about their child's needs, and are clearly using the custody issue as a battleground. As the film continues, however, we see a change taking place. Both parents begin to realize that each loves and cares about their child. They reestablish respect for each other and start thinking about their son's best interest. Unfortunately, though the film is thought-provoking, it leaves us with the idea that custody is a win or lose proposition. Streep and Hoffman see only one option—sole custody. This is unfortunate because by the end of the film we have a family for whom joint custody might be a satisfying and appropriate option. We see a child who loves and wants contact with both parents, and two capable, loving parents who are well on their way to separating their marital issues from the tasks of parenting. When we saw the film we couldn't help wonder why it didn't end with the couple deciding upon joint custody. The reason may well be that many moviegoers might have been dissatisfied and thought "that's a typical Hollywood ending, it just doesn't happen like that in everyday life." We hope this book has made it clear that it could.

Once again, joint custody is a legal means of insuring that divorced parents have the right to actively participate in their child's upbringing. The success or failure of such an arrangement depends to a great extent on the parents' commitment to make it work. Joint custody has opened up a number of potential options which, along with traditional sole custody, give divorcing parents a greater opportunity to fully consider the needs of their family. Parents can now choose from these whatever custody alternative best suits their family's practical and emotional requirements. In doing so, they are likely to make a choice which will offer continued maximum satisfaction to the entire family.

Suggested Readings

The following are books which may be useful to divorcing families. This list is not exhaustive and does not necessarily imply endorsement of the authors' ideas.

Andrew, Jan. *Divorce and the American Family*. New York: Franklin Watts, 1978.
   The author discusses the history and legal status of divorce, divorce reform, divorce's effect on adults and children, remarriage and alternative lifestyles. The author concludes by examining the future of the family as an institution.
Atkin, Edith, and Rubin, Estelle. *Part-Time Father*. New York: New American Library, 1976.
   This book focuses on the relationship between the separated or divorced father and his children. The authors offer practical suggestions for dealing with some of the situations faced by divorced fathers, such as informing children, visitation, dating, remarriage, etc. They also discuss custodial fathers and divided custody arrangements. The authors argue that divided custody is generally too disruptive for the child.
Bass, Howard L., and Rein, M. L. *Divorce or Marriage: A Legal Guide*. New York: Prentice-Hall, 1974.
   This book offers the reader answers to many legal questions in marriage, divorce, and custody. In the section on custody, the authors suggest parents sign a written agreement contain-

ing provisions intended to help minimize the negative effects of divorce on children.

Folberg, Jay H., and Graham, Marva. "Joint Custody of Children Following Divorce." *12 University of California–Davis Law Review,* Symposium Issue on Children and the Law (Spring 1979).

This extremely well-researched article covers legal, social, and psychological aspects of joint custody. It will be especially valuable for legal and mental health professionals involved in child custody cases.

Forman, Lynn. *Getting It Together—The Divorced Mother's Guide.* New York: Berkley Medallion Books, 1974.

A practical guide for divorced women on "getting it together" after divorce. It deals with issues related to emotions, children, careers, dating, friendships, and living together.

Galper, Miriam. *Co-Parenting—Sharing Your Child Equally.* Philadelphia: Running Press, 1978.

A very readable account of the author's personal and professional experience with co-parenting. This book provides concrete advice about how to develop and maintain a co-parenting arrangement. Co-parenting encompasses a number of different moral and legal arrangements.

Gardner, Richard A. *The Boys and Girls Book about Divorce.* New York: Bantam Books, 1970.

An excellent book for children in middle school through early adolescence. The author talks directly to children about the fears and problems they may face following their parents' divorce. He offers straightforward ideas about how to deal with mother's dating, visiting with father, finding out if parents love you, getting along with stepparents, and feeling bad or ashamed. The book is a good means for facilitating further discussion between parents and children about divorce.

Goldstein, Joseph; Freud, Anna; and Solnit, Albert J. *Beyond the Best Interests of the Child.* New York: Free Press, 1973.

This is an influential book written from a psychoanalytical perspective which discusses child custody, foster placement, and adoption. The authors emphasize the importance of maintaining continuity in a child's relationship and surroundings. A number of the arguments against joint custody have come from ideas discussed in this book.

Hamilton, Marshall L. *Fathers' Influence on Children.* Chicago: Nelson-Hall, 1977.

This book reviews relevant research concerning the influence of fathers on children. The author emphasizes the need for recognition and examination of the father's contribution to parenting.

Hazen, Barbara Shook. *Two Homes to Live In: A Child's-Eye View of Divorce.* New York: Human Sciences Press, 1978.
This is a book divorced parents could read and discuss with their young children. It talks about the benefits and problems of living in two homes.

Krantzler, Mel. *Creative Divorce.* New York: New American Library, 1974.
A well-known book that views divorce as an opportunity for personal growth. The author describes the divorce process, and offers guidelines for adjusting to and profiting from this experience.

Lamb, Michael, ed. *The Role of the Father in Child Development.* New York: John Wiley, 1976.
A collection of articles dealing with the role of the father in child development. The articles focus on the effects fathers' have on the psychological development of children.

Maddox, Brenda. *The Half-Parent.* New York: M. Evans, 1975.
An examination of the situations and problems encountered by stepparents. The author includes relevant information from her own experiences as a stepparent.

Noble, June and Noble, William. *The Custody Trap.* New York: Hawthorn Books, 1975.
This book discusses problems inherent in the present custody system. It uses case examples in a very readable fashion to illustrate the adversary nature of custody decision making. The authors conclude with a recommendation of joint responsibility for children following marital dissolution.

Richards, Arlene, and Willis, Irene. *How to Get It Together When Your Parents Are Coming Apart.* New York: David McKay, 1976.
A book intended for teenagers and persons interested in helping young people cope with parental separation. It deals with situations and feelings teenagers experience before, during, and after divorce. The last chapter discusses when and where to seek professional help.

Roman, Mel, and Haddad, William. *The Disposable Parent— The Case for Joint Custody.* New York: Holt, Rinehart and Winston, 1978.

These two authors assert that fathers have been treated like "disposable parents." Written for both professionals and parents, the authors believe that joint custody should be not merely an option for divorcing families, but rather the judicial presumption.

Shepard, Morris A., and Goldman, Gerald. *Divorced Dads— Their Kids, Ex-wives and New Lives.* Radnor, Penn.: Chilton Book Co., 1979.
An interesting and informative book for divorced fathers. It urges fathers to remain involved in their children's lives following divorce, and offers practical suggestions for doing so. Both of the authors discuss their own experiences of sharing with former wives the care and responsibility for children. Other pertinent issues include how to negotiate with your former spouse, plan a new social life, arrange a career, and emotionally and financially adjust to divorce.

Singleton, Mary Ann. *Life After Marriage—Divorce as a New Beginning.* New York: Stein and Day, 1974.
A guide to help women through the divorce process. The author offers practical suggestions and advice on many subjects. She encourages divorced women to develop their own sense of identity and independence. Divorce is viewed as an opportunity for personal growth.

Victor, Ira, and Winkler, Win Ann. *Fathers and Custody.* New York: Hawthorn Books, 1977.
The authors describe the father's role in different custody arrangements and include a chapter on joint custody. Other issues related to fathers and custody are also discussed. The appendix lists three types of resources: divorced fathers groups, single-parent and child-help groups, and legal advice referrals.

References

BOOKS AND ARTICLES

Abarbanel, A. R. Shared parenting after separation and divorce: a study of joint custody. *American Journal of Orthopsychiatry,* April 1979, *49* (2), 320–29.

Aguilera, D. C., and Messick, Janice M. *Crisis Intervention— Theory and Methodology.* St. Louis: C. V. Mosby, 1974.

Ahrons, C. R. The binuclear family: two households, one family. *Alternative Lifestyles,* 1979, 2 (4), 499–515.

Ahrons, C. R. Joint custody arrangements in the post-divorce family. *Journal of Divorce,* 1980, *3* (3), 189–205.

Alexander, S. J. Protecting the child's rights in custody cases. *Family Coordinator,* 1977, *26,* 377–82.

Anderson, R. E. Where's dad? Parental deprivation and delinquency. *Archives of General Psychiatry,* 1968, *18,* 641–49.

Andrew, J. *Divorce and the American Family.* New York: Franklin Watts, 1978.

Anno: Children—Alternate Custody. *American Law Reports Annotated,* Vol. 92, 2nd Series (92 ALR 2d), 1963, pp. 695–745.

Anthony, E. J. Children at risk from divorce: A review. In E. J. Anthony and C. Koupernik (eds.), *The Child in His Family: Children at Psychiatric Risk.* New York: John Wiley and Sons, 1974.

Atkin, E., and Rubin, E. *Part-Time Father.* New York: New American Library, 1977.

Bass, H. L., and Rein, M. L. *Divorce or Marriage: A Legal Guide.* New York: Prentice-Hall, 1974.

Baum, C. The best of both parents. *New York Times Magazine,* Oct. 31, 1976, 44–46.

Bem, S. Psychological androgyny. In Alice G. Sargent, *Beyond Sex Roles.* St. Paul: West Publishing Co., 1977.

Bondehagen, K. E. Joint Custody of Children and the Wisconsin Divorce Reform Act of 1977. Unpublished paper, Dec. 1977.

Brandwein, R. A.; Brown, C. A.; and Fox, E. M. The social situation of divorced mothers and their families. *Journal of Marriage and the Family,* Aug. 1974, *36,* 498–514.

Brown, C. A.; Feldberg, R.; Fox, E. M.; and Kohen, J. Divorce: Chance of a new lifetime. *Journal of Social Issues,* 1976, *32* (1), 119–33.

Caplan, G. *Principles of Preventive Psychiatry.* New York: Basic Books, 1964.

Caplan, M. G., and Douglas, V. Incidence of parental loss in children with depressed mood. *Journal of Child Psychology and Psychiatry,* 1969, *10,* 225–32.

Deckard, B. S. *The Women's Movement: Political, Socio-economic, and Psychological Issues.* New York and London: Harper and Row, 1975.

The deep discontent of the working woman. *Business Week,* Feb. 9, 1979, 28.

Demeter, A. *Legal Kidnapping—What Happens to a Family When the Father Kidnaps Two Children.* Boston: Beacon Press, 1977.

Derdeyn, A. P. Child custody consultation. *American Journal of Orthopsychiatry,* 1975, *15,* 791–801.

Derdeyn, A. P. Children in divorce: Intervention in the phase of separation. *Pediatrics,* July 1977, *60* (1), 20–27.

Despert, L. J. *Children of Divorce.* New York: Doubleday, 1962.

Douglas, J. W. B. Broken families and child behavior. *Journal Royal College of Physicians,* London, 1970, *4,* 203–10.

Dullea, G. Joint custody—Is sharing the child a dangerous idea? *New York Times,* May 24, 1976, p. 24.

Dullea, G. Half-time fathers know best. *Chicago Tribune,* March 19, 1978, Section 5, p. 6.

Eder, V. Shared custody—An idea whose time has come. *Conciliation Courts Review,* 1978, *16* (1), 23–25.

Eisler, R. T. *Dissolution: No-Fault Divorce, Marriage and the Future of Women.* New York: McGraw-Hill, 1977.

Elkin, M. Reflection on joint custody and family law, *Conciliation Courts Review*, 1978, *16* (3), 16–19.

Erikson, E. H. *Childhood and Society*. New York: W. W. Norton, 1963.

Felner, R. D.; Stolberg, A.; and Cowen, E. L. Crisis events and school mental health referral patterns of young children. *Journal of Consulting and Clinical Psychology*, 1975, *43* (3), 305–10.

Flavell, J. H. *The Developmental Psychology of Jean Piaget*. Princeton: Van Nostrand, 1963.

Folberg, J. H., and Graham, M. Joint custody of children following divorce. *12 University of California–Davis Law Review*, Spring 1979.

Forman, L. *Getting It Together—The Divorced Mother's Guide*. New York: Berkley Medallion Books, 1974.

Foster, H. H., and Freed, D. J. Life with father: 1978. *Family Law Quarterly*, 1978, *11* (4), 321–42.

Fraiberg, S. H. *The Magic Years—Understanding and Handling the Problems of Early Childhood*. New York: Charles Scribner's Sons, 1959.

Freed, D. J., and Foster, H. H. Divorce in the fifty states: An outline. *Family Law Quarterly*, 1977, *11* (3), 297–313.

Freud, A. Adolescence, *Psychoanalytic Study of the Child*. 1958, *13*, 255–78.

Gaddis, S. M. Joint Custody of children: A divorce decision-making alternative. *Conciliation Courts Review*, 1978, *16* (1), 17–22.

Galper, M. *Co-parenting—Sharing your child equally*. Philadelphia: Running Press, 1978.

Gardner, R. A. *The Boys and Girls Book about Divorce*. New York: Bantom Books, 1970.

Goldstein, J.; Freud, A.; and Solnit, A. J. *Before the Best Interests of the Child*. New York and London: Free Press, 1979.

Goldstein, J.; Freud, A.; and Solnit, A. J. *Beyond the Best Interests of the Child*. New York and London: Free Press, 1973.

Grief, J. B. Fathers, children and joint custody. *American Journal of Orthopsychiatry*, April 1979, *49* (2), 311–19.

Gunn, S. Divorce court 'ERA': Women paying support. *Chicago Tribune*, July 30, 1978.

Hamilton, M. L. *Fathers' Influence on Children*. Chicago: Nelson-Hall Co., 1977.

Happy daddies—The case for half-time fathers. *Human Behavior*, Nov. 1978, *1* (11), 37.

Hazen, B. S. *Two Homes to Live In: A Child's-Eye View of Divorce.* New York: Human Sciences Press, 1978.

Hetherington, E. M.; Cox, M.; and Cox, R. Divorced fathers. *The Family Coordinator,* 1976, *25,* 417–28.

Horowitz, J. A., and Perdue, B. J. Single-parent families. *Nursing Clinics of North America,* Sept. 1977, *12* (3), 503–11.

Jenkins, R. L. Maxims in child custody cases. *The Family Coordinator,* 1977, *26* (4), 385–89.

Johnson, S. "Divorced fathers organizing." *New York Times,* Feb. 14, 1978.

Kellogg, M. A. "Joint custody." *Newsweek,* Jan. 24, 1977, 56–57.

Kelly, J. B., and Wallerstein, J. S. The effects of parental divorce: Experiences of the child in early latency. *American Journal of Orthopsychiatry,* Jan. 1976, *46* (1), 20–32.

Keshet, H. F., and Rosenthal, K. M. Fathering after marital separation. *Social Work,* 1978, *23* (1), 11–18.

Kessler, S. *The American Way of Divorce: Prescriptions for Change.* Chicago: Nelson-Hall, 1975.

Klebanow, S. Parenting in the single parent family. *Journal of the American Academy of Psychoanalysis,* 1976, *4* (1), 37–48.

Krantzler, M. *Creative Divorce.* New York: New American Library, 1974.

Lamb, M. (ed.), *The Role of the Father in Child Development.* New York: John Wiley, 1976.

Lawrence, W. Divided custody of children after their parents divorce. *Journal of Family Law,* 1968, *8,* 58–68.

Levine, J. A. *Who Will Raise the Children?—New Options for Fathers (and Mothers).* Philadelphia: Lippincott, 1976.

Luepnitz, D. A. Which aspects of divorce affect childen? *The Family Coordinator,* 1979, *28* (1), 79–85.

Maddox, B. *The Half-Parent.* New York: M. Evans, 1975.

McDermott, J. F. Divorce and its psychiatric sequelae in children. *Archives of General Psychiatry,* 1970, *23* (5), 421–27.

Mendes, H. A. Single fathers. *The Family Coordinator,* 1976, *25,* 439–49.

Morrison, J. R. Parental divorce as a factor in childhood psychiatric illness. *Comprehensive Psychiatry,* March-April 1974, *15* (2), 95–101.

Myricks, N. The equal rights amendment: Its potential impact on family life. *Family Coordinator,* 1977, *26,* 321–26.

Napier, A., with Whitaker, C. *The Family Crucible.* New York: Harper and Row, 1978.

Nehls, N. M. *Joint custody of children: a descriptive study.*

Portland: The Association of Family Conciliation Courts, 1979.

Nehls, N. M. and Morgenbesser, M. Joint custody: an exploration of the issues. *Family Process,* 1980, *19,* 117–25.

Noble, J. and Noble, W. *The Custody Trap.* New York: Hawthorn Books, 1975.

One child, two homes. *Time,* Jan. 27, 1979, 61.

Orthner, D. K.; Brown, T.; and Ferguson, D. Single-parent fatherhood: An emerging family life style. *The Family Coordinator,* 1976, *25,* 429–37.

Richards, A., and Willis, I. *How to Get It Together When Your Parents Are Coming Apart.* New York: David McKay, 1976.

Roberts, A. R., and Roberts, B. J. Divorce and the child: A pyrrhic victory? In A. R. Roberts (ed.), *Childhood Deprivation.* Springfield: Charles C. Thomas, 1974.

Roman, M. The disposable parent. *Conciliation Courts Review,* 1977, *15* (2), 1–11.

Roman, M., and Haddad, W. The case for joint custody. *Psychology Today,* Sept. 1978, 96–97, 99–105.

Roman, M., and Haddad, W. *The Disposable Parent—The Case for Joint Custody.* New York: Holt, Rinehart and Winston, 1978.

Rutter, M. Parent-child separation: Psychological effects on the children. *Journal of Child Psychology and Psychiatry.* 1971, *12,* 233–60.

Santrock, J. W. Influence of onset and type of paternal absence on the first four eriksonian developmental crises. *Developmental Psychology,* 1970, *3* (2), 273–74.

Santrock, J. W. Relation of type and onset of father absence in cognitive development. *Child Development,* June 1972, *43* (2), 455–69.

Sargent, A. G. *Beyond Sex Roles.* St. Paul: West Publishing Co., 1977.

Shavin, S. *Joint Parenting after Divorce: An Alternative to Traditional Child Custody.* Master's thesis, California School of Professional Psychology, 1976. In M. Roman and W. Haddad, *The Disposable Parent—The Case for Joint Custody.* New York: Holt, Rinehart and Winston, 1978.

Shepard, M. A., and Goldman, G. *Divorced Dads—Their Kids, Ex-Wives and New Lives.* Radnor, Pa.: Chilton Book Co., 1979.

Sheresky, N., and Mannes, M. *Uncoupling—The Art of Coming Apart.* New York: Viking Press, 1972.

Singleton, M. A. *Life after Marriage—Divorce as a New Beginning.* New York: Stein and Day, 1974.

Sorosky, A. D. The psychological effects of divorce on adolescents. *Adolescence,* 1977, *12* (45), 125–36.

A Statistical Portrait of Women in the United States, April 1976. United States Department of Commerce, Bureau of the Census, Census Tracts, 1970.

Sugar, M. Children of divorce. *Pediatrics, October* 1970, *46* (4), 588–95. (a)

Sugar, M. Divorce and children. *Southern Medical Journal,* Dec. 1970, *63* (12), 1458–61. (b)

Truesdell Cox, M. J., and Cease, L. Joint custody—What does it mean? How does it work? *Family Advocate,* Aug. 1978, 10–13, 42–44.

United States Statistical Abstract. United States Bureau of the Census, Washington, D.C., 1977.

United States Vital Statistics Report. D.H.E.W. Publications, Dec. 12, 1977, *25* (13), 13.

Van Gelder, L. New study favors joint custody. *New York Times,* Jan. 26, 1979.

Victor, I., and Winkler, W. A. *Fathers and Custody.* New York: Hawthorn Books, 1977.

Wallerstein, J. S., and Kelly, J. B. The effects of parental divorce: The adolescent experience. In E. J. Anthony and C. Koupernik (eds.), *The Child in His Family—Children at Psychiatric Risk.* New York: John Wiley, 1974.

Wallerstein, J. S., and Kelly, J. B. The effects of parental divorce—Experiences of the preschool child. *Journal of the American Academy of Child Psychiatry,* 1975, *14* (4), 600–616.

Wallerstein, J. S., and Kelly, J. B. The effects of parental divorce: Experiences of the child in latency. *American Journal of Orthopsychiatry.* April 1976, *46* (2), 256–69.

Ware, C. Joint custody: One way to end the war. *New West,* Feb. 26, 1979, 42–55.

Westman, J. C. Effect of divorce on a child's personality development. *Medical Aspects of Human Sexuality.* Jan. 1972, *6* (1), 38–55.

Wheller, M. *No-Fault Divorce.* Boston: Beacon Press, 1974.

Yuenger, J. Child-snatching: Tragic outgrowth of soaring divorce. *Chicago Tribune,* March 26, 1978.

COURT CASES

Braiman v. *Braiman* 4 Fam. L. Rep. 2522 (N.Y.C. Ct. App. 1978).

Davis v. *Davis* 354 S.W. 2d 526 (Springfield Ct. App. 1962).

Dodd v. *Dodd* 4 Fam. L. Rep. 2302 (N.Y. Cty. Sup. Ct. 1978).

Gall v. *Gall* 336 So. 2d 10 (Fla. App. 1976).

Krois v. *Krois* 4 Fam. L. Rep. 2017 (N.Y. Sup. Ct. Queens Div. 1977).

Levy v. *Levy* 2 Fam. L. Rep. 2228 (N.Y. Sup. Ct. N.Y., 1/29/76).

Lumbra v. *Lumbra* 5 Fam. L. Rep. 2169 (Vermont Sup. Ct. 1978).

Mullen v. *Mullen* 49 S.E. 2d 349 (App. Div. 1948).

1 Fam. L. Rep. 2708 (8-26-78).

Perroti v. *Perroti* 355 N.Y.S. 2d 68.

Salk v. *Salk* 393 N.Y.S. 2d 841 (1977).

Utley v. *Utley* 3 Fam. L. Rep. 2047 (D.C. Ct. App. 1976).

Winn v. *Winn* 299 P. 2d 721 (Dist. Ct. App. 1st Dist. Div. 2 1956).

Wood v. *Wood* 400 S.W. 2d 421 (St. Louis Ct. App. 1966).

Index